# LUCY'S FARMHOUSE KITCHEN
## RECIPES FROM THE DEWBERRY FARM MYSTERIES

### KAREN MACINERNEY

GRAY WHALE PRESS

Copyright © 2019 by Karen MacInerney

All rights reserved.

No part of this book may be reproduced in any form or by any electronic or mechanical means, including information storage and retrieval systems, without written permission from the author, except for the use of brief quotations in a book review.

Names, characters, places, and incidents in this book are either products of the author's imagination or used fictitiously. Any resemblance to actual events or locales or persons, living or dead, is entirely coincidental.

**Books in the Dewberry Farm Mystery Series**

*Killer Jam*

*Fatal Frost*

*Deadly Brew*

*Mistletoe Murder*

*Dyeing Season*

*Wicked Harvest*

❦ Created with Vellum

CONTENTS

*Introduction* vii

SNACKS AND APPETIZERS
German Pretzels 3
Dewberry Farm Shrimp and Goat Cheese Quesadillas 6
Seven- (or Six-) Layer Dip 8
Fire-Roasted Salsa 10
Guacamole 12

MAIN DISHES
King Ranch Chicken Casserole 15
Rosita's Tamales 17
Christmas Pork Posole 19
Hoppin' John 21
Easy Chicken or Turkey Enchiladas Verde 23
Alfie's Smoked Pork Ribs 25
Chicken and Dumplings, Southern Style 27

SIDE DISHES
German Potato Salad 33
Texas Caviar 35

BREADS AND ROLLS
Quinn's Famous Glazed Maple Twists 39
Quinn's Vanocka (Czech Christmas Bread) 42
Quinn's Blue Onion Mazanec 45
Sweet Texas Cornbread 47

DESSERTS
Buttercup Pecan Pie 51
Texas Peach Cobbler 53
Bienenstich (Bee Sting Cake) 55

Goat Milk Flan 58
Fresh Strawberry Custard Pie 60
Grandma Vogel's Lebkuchen Bars 62
Halloween Pumpkin Bars 65
Lucy's Apple Dumplings 67
Grandma Vogel's Snickerdoodles 69
Almond Crescent Cookies 71
Lebkuchen (Gingerbread) Oktoberfest Hearts 73
Chocolate Glazed Lebkuchen 75

CANDIES
Texas Pecan Pralines 81
Brown Sugar Fudge Balls 83
Caramel Turtles 86
Candy Cane Fudge 88
Butterscotch Squares 90

BEVERAGES
Bubba Allen's Glühwein (Mulled Wine) 95
Texas Sweet Tea 97
Mulled Honey Wine 99
The Hitching Post's Tom & Jerrys 101
Dewberry Margaritas 103

SAUCES
Verde Sauce 107
Red Chili Sauce 109

JAMS
Killer Dewberry Jam 113
Spiced Pumpkin Butter 115
Spiced Pear Jam 117

CHEESES
Grandma Vogel's Cottage Cheese 121
Farm-fresh Mozzarella Cheese 123

CRAFTS

| | |
|---|---|
| Mason Jar Beeswax Candles | 129 |
| Mary Jane's Lavender Goat Milk Soap | 131 |
| Natural Easter Egg Dyes | 133 |
| Honey Lip Balm | 135 |
| Grandma Vogel's Lavender Bath Salts | 136 |

KITCHEN TIPS
| | |
|---|---|
| Lucy's Handy Kitchen Tips | 139 |

GARDEN TIPS
| | |
|---|---|
| Lucy and Grandma Vogel's Garden Tips | 143 |
| Grandma Vogel's Garlic-Pepper Tea | 149 |
| Sneak Peek: Killer Jam | 151 |
| *More Books by Karen MacInerney* | 159 |
| *Acknowledgments* | 161 |
| *About the Author* | 163 |

# INTRODUCTION

Thank you so much for picking up a copy of Lucy's Farmhouse Kitchen!

Here, you'll find all the recipes from the first six Dewberry Farm mysteries, as well as the recipes from Slay Bells Ring (a Dewberry Farm novella). I've also added several other dishes I love and that are typical of the part of Texas I've lived in for more than twenty years. The book just didn't seem complete without recipes for enchiladas, Hoppin' John, cornbread, Texas caviar, guacamole, and King Ranch chicken casserole (and that's just for starters). I have lots more local favorites in my recipe file too; you'll see them in future books, I promise!

Each region has its own cuisine. Although I grew up in the Northeast and, when I first moved to Texas, found even mild salsa tastebud-annihilating, I've come to love spicy food and to embrace several traditional Texas dishes as part of my permanent repertoire. It's been fun collecting them here, and I hope you enjoy them as much as I do.

I've also added some bonus kitchen and garden tips from Lucy and her Grandma Vogel, including a great garlic-pepper tea recipe that will send your garden pests running.

I've long dreamed of writing a series based in the part of Texas

## INTRODUCTION

Buttercup is found in, ever since visiting family friends Maryann and Clovis Heimsath at their farm in Fayetteville, Texas two decades ago. I fell in love with the place immediately, and have been enamored of it ever since.

It's been wonderful to see that long-ago dream come to fruition, and I cannot thank you all enough for your support of Lucy, Tobias, Quinn, and the rest of the gang (both human and animal) in Buttercup. None of this would exist without you.

XXX OOO

Karen

# SNACKS AND APPETIZERS

# GERMAN PRETZELS

## WICKED HARVEST, BOOK 6

INGREDIENTS:

*Pretzels*

- 4 cups all-purpose flour
- 2 teaspoons salt
- 1 teaspoon sugar
- 1 cup lukewarm water
- 4 1/2 teaspoons (2 pkgs) active dry yeast
- 3 tbsp butter
- Coarse salt for sprinkling

*Baking Soda Bath*

- 1/2 cup baking soda
- 2 quarts water

## DIRECTIONS:

1. In a small bowl, dissolve the yeast in the lukewarm water. In a large mixing bowl, combine flour and salt. Form a well in the middle of the flour mixture. Add the sugar to the center of the well, then pour the yeast mixture into the well. Let rest for 15 minutes before mixing.
2. After 15 minutes, add the softened butter to the mixing bowl and knead everything to a smooth dough by hand or with the dough hook on a standing mixer, adding a bit more water (not too much) if dough is too dry. Form dough into a ball and let dough rest for 30 minutes.
3. Line a cookie sheet with parchment paper. Cut the ball of dough into twelve equal parts, then with your hands, roll each piece on an unfloured, clean table or countertop to a dough rope of about 20 inches (not less), tapering the dough at the ends. Try not to overwork the dough; if it gets too warm as you roll it out, it might tear.
4. To form a pretzel shape, place a dough rope on the parchment-lined cookie sheet so that it creates a letter "U". Take both ends of the "U" and cross them over each other twice to form a twist, then bring the twist down and place it over the bottom curve of the "U".
5. Place the pretzels in the refrigerator (I like to put them on parchment-paper-lined pans that I later use for baking), uncovered, for about an hour.
6. Preheat the oven to 400 F. Fill a large pot with water until 3/4 full and bring the water to a boil. Carefully and slowly add the baking soda to the boiling water; stand back a bit, as the baking soda will bubble up violently for a moment when it hits the water.
7. Using a slotted spoon, gently drop each pretzel into the bath for ten seconds, then turn the pretzel over for another ten

seconds. Place the finished pretzels on a baking sheet lined with parchment paper.
8. Score each pretzel once with a razor blade or sharp knife and sprinkle with coarse salt. Bake the pretzels for about 15 to 20 minutes, depending on how dark you like them.

# DEWBERRY FARM SHRIMP AND GOAT CHEESE QUESADILLAS

## DYEING SEASON, BOOK 5

INGREDIENTS:

- 1/2 pound medium shrimp, unpeeled
- 4 ounces goat cheese
- 1 cup grated Monterey Jack cheese
- 2 tablespoons cilantro, minced
- 1/2 teaspoon fresh garlic, minced
- 1/2 teaspoon salt
- 1/4 teaspoon black pepper

DIRECTIONS:

1. Fill a medium saucepan half full of water. Bring to a boil and add shrimp; stir once, and cook for three minutes.
2. Drain and set aside until cool, then peel shrimp and chop coarsely.
3. In a medium mixing bowl, combine goat cheese, Monterey Jack cheese, cilantro, garlic, salt, pepper and shrimp.

ASSEMBLY

- 1 recipe Quesadilla filling
- 8 flour tortillas
- 4 teaspoons butter, divided
- 1 cup Verde Sauce

1. Lay four flour tortillas out on a countertop and place one fourth of filling on each tortilla. Spread filling evenly over the entire tortilla and place one of the remaining tortillas on top of filling. Press firmly. Repeat with remaining tortillas and filling.
2. Melt one teaspoon butter in a medium non-stick pan over medium heat. Place one quesadilla in skillet and cook for 3 minutes on each side. Hold in a 200 degree oven until ready to serve. Repeat with remaining butter and quesadillas. Cut each quesadilla into quarters with a pizza cutter. Serve with salsa verde.

Note: Use extra verde sauce for enchiladas or as a dip for chips!

# SEVEN- (OR SIX-) LAYER DIP

## DEWBERRY FARM BONUS RECIPE

INGREDIENTS:

- 1 (16- ounce) can refried beans, pinto or black, with or without jalapenos
- 1 (8-ounce) container sour cream
- 1 (1-ounce) package taco seasoning mix (or several shakes from a jar of taco seasoning, to taste)
- 4 plum or medium on-the-vine tomatoes, diced
- 1 bunch green onions, finely chopped (green and white)
- Guacamole (per guacamole recipe, or see note below)
- 2 cups shredded cheddar, Colby jack or Mexican-style cheese blend
- 1 (2.25-ounce) can black olives – drained and finely chopped (optional–I don't like black olives, so I never use them, which is why my dip usually has a mere 6 layers)

DIRECTIONS:

1. In a 9×13 inch dish or on a large serving platter, spread the refried beans.
2. In a small bowl, blend the sour cream and taco seasoning. Spread over the refried beans.
3. In a medium bowl, mash the avocados, then mix in lime juice, cilantro, pico de gallo or salsa, garlic salt and pepper. Spread this over the sour cream mixture.
4. Top with tomatoes, green onions, shredded cheese, and black olives if you're really going for 7 layers (I never do).
5. Serve with tortilla chips. Lots of them.

**On Guacamole and Pico de Gallo...**

If I have it on hand, quickly chop up a plum tomato or two, add a small handful of diced onion, chop up about 1/4-1/3 of a jalapeno, and squeeze in 1/2-1 lime, then add a bit of chopped cilantro and some garlic salt. To make guacamole, you can use the guacamole recipe I've included, or I often just mix some of this this with mashed avocado to make on-the-fly guacamole, with a bit more lime juice and salt to taste. (When I am lazy or my pantry is bare, I just use salsa.)

# FIRE-ROASTED SALSA

## DEWBERRY FARM BONUS RECIPE

I learned a version of this recipe from my friend Antonia Alvarado many years ago; she liked it with her homemade tamales, but it is also terrific with chips as an appetizer, on tacos, or in any number of other applications!

INGREDIENTS:

- 4-5 large Roma tomatoes, whole, not cored or cut
- 2 cloves garlic (skin on)
- 1 large serrano or jalapeño pepper
- 1/4 cup minced onion
- 1 teaspoon salt, or to taste
- 1/2 bunch cilantro

DIRECTIONS:

1. Put a piece of aluminum foil in a heavy pan over medium-high heat.

2. Place the uncut tomatoes, garlic, and pepper in the pan. Roast until they are charred on all sides and and soft, removing items as they are done (smaller items will cook faster).
3. Peel the garlic and remove the stem from the pepper, then put the tomatoes, pepper, and garlic in a food processor. Add the onion, salt, and cilantro and process until the salsa is smooth. Add more salt or cilantro to taste.

# GUACAMOLE

## DEWBERRY FARM BONUS RECIPE

INGREDIENTS:

- 3 medium ripe avocados
- 2 garlic cloves, minced
- 1/2 teaspoon salt
- 2 tomatoes, chopped
- 1 small onion, diced
- 1 jalapeno, finely diced
- 1 to 2 tablespoons lime juice (to taste)
- 1/8-1/4 cup minced fresh cilantro (to taste)

DIRECTIONS:

1. Mash avocados with garlic and salt.
2. Stir in remaining ingredients, adjusting to taste. Serve with tortilla chips, on top of tacos, as an accompaniment to enchiladas, with quesadillas… or even just with a spoon.

# MAIN DISHES

# KING RANCH CHICKEN CASSEROLE

## DEWBERRY FARM BONUS RECIPE

Is there any better way to use up all that extra holiday turkey? I think not! (Except maybe Enchiladas Verde... read on!) I love this with guacamole and sour cream on the side, for extra deliciousness (and calories).

INGREDIENTS:

- 1 chopped green bell pepper
- 1 chopped onion
- 2 tablespoons olive oil
- 2 cups chopped cooked chicken or turkey
- 1 can cream of chicken soup
- 1 can cream of mushroom soup
- 1 can Ro-Tel diced tomato and green chiles
- 1 teaspoon chili powder
- 1/4 teaspoon salt
- 2 pinches garlic powder
- a few dashes cayenne pepper (optional)
- 1/4 teaspoon black pepper

- 12 corn tortillas, torn into 1-inch pieces
- 2 cups grated cheddar, Monterrey Jack or Mexican-blend cheese

DIRECTIONS:

1. Preheat oven to 350°. In a large skillet over medium-high heat, sauté bell pepper and onion in olive oil until tender (around 5 minutes). Stir in chicken, bell pepper, onion, chicken or turkey, cream of chicken soup, cream of mushroom soup, Ro-Tel, chili powder, salt, garlic powder, optional cayenne pepper, and black pepper; remove from heat.
2. Layer one-third of torn tortillas in the bottom of a lightly greased 13- x 9-inch baking dish. Top with one-third of chicken mixture and 2/3 cup cheese. Repeat layers twice, finishing with cheese. Bake for 30 to 35 minutes, or until bubbly and cheese is melted.
3. Serve with sour cream or crema and/or guacamole on the side for extra decadence.

# ROSITA'S TAMALES

## MISTLETOE MURDER, BOOK 4

Tamales are a traditional Christmas food in Mexico and much of Texas, but I love eating them anytime, especially with fire-roasted salsa on the side. You can get masa harina and corn husks everywhere in Texas, but may have to order them online elsewhere.

INGREDIENTS:

- 3½ pounds pork shoulder or 3½ pounds pork butt, trimmed of fat and cut up
- 10 cups water
- 1 medium onion, quartered
- 3 garlic cloves, minced
- 3½ teaspoons salt
- 4 cups red chili sauce (see recipe in "Sauces")
- ¾ cup shortening
- 6 cups masa harina
- 1½ teaspoons baking powder
- 50 dried corn husks (about 8 inches long)

## DIRECTIONS:

1. In a 5-quart Dutch oven, bring pork, water, onion, garlic, and 1½ teaspoons salt to boil and simmer, covered, about 2½ hours, or until meat is very tender. Remove meat from broth and allow both meat and broth to cool. Shred the meat using 2 forks, discarding fat, then strain the broth and reserve 6 cups.
2. In a large saucepan, heat the red chili sauce and add meat; simmer, covered, for 10 minutes.
3. To make masa, beat shortening on medium speed in a large bowl for 1 minute. In a separate bowl, stir together masa harina, baking powder, and 2 teaspoons salt. Add masa harina mixture and broth to shortening alternately, beating well after each addition. (Add just enough broth to make a thick, creamy paste.)
4. In the meantime, soak corn husks in warm water for at least 20 minutes; rinse to remove any corn silk and drain well.
5. To assemble each tamale, spread 2 tablespoons of the masa mixture on the center of the corn husk. (Each husk should be 8 inches long and 6 inches wide at the top. If a husk is small, overlap 2 small ones to form one. If it is large, tear a strip from the side.)
6. Place about 1 tablespoon meat and sauce mixture in the middle of the masa, then fold in the sides of husk and fold up the bottom.
7. Place a steamer basket in a large pot and put the tamales in the basket, open side up. Add water to pot so that the level is just below the basket. Bring water to boil and reduce heat. Cover and steam 40 minutes, adding water when necessary.
8. To freeze, leave tamales in the husks and place them in freezer bags. To reheat, thaw and wrap in a wet paper towel and reheat in the microwave for 2 minutes for 1 or 2 or resteam them just until hot.

# CHRISTMAS PORK POSOLE

## MISTLETOE MURDER, BOOK 4

INGREDIENTS:

- 4 medium onions, divided
- 7 tablespoons canola oil or vegetable oil, divided
- 4½ tablespoons ancho chile powder, divided
- 3 tablespoons dried oregano (preferably Mexican), divided
- 1 6- to 6½-pound bone-in pork shoulder (Boston butt), cut into 4- to 5-inch pieces, some meat left on bone
- 5 cups (or more) low-salt chicken broth
- 4 7-ounce cans diced green chiles, drained
- 5 large garlic cloves, minced
- 4 teaspoons ground cumin
- 4 15-ounce cans golden or white hominy, drained
- 1 – 2 cups red chili sauce (see recipe in Sauces section, or use pre-prepared)
- 4 limes, each cut into 4 wedges
- Thinly sliced green onion
- Chopped fresh cilantro

- Tortilla shells or chips, head of cabbage (chopped), 5–10 radishes (thinly sliced), all optional for garnish at end.

DIRECTIONS:

1. Preheat oven to 350°F. Thinly slice 2 onions. Heat 4 tablespoons oil in heavy large ovenproof pot over medium-high heat, then add sliced onions to pot and sauté until onions begin to soften, about 3 minutes. Add 1½ tablespoons ancho chile powder and 1½ tablespoons oregano and stir to coat. Sprinkle pork with salt and add to pot. Add 5 cups broth. Bring to boil. Cover and transfer to oven.
2. Braise pork until tender enough to shred easily, about 2 hours. Using slotted spoon, transfer pork to large bowl and pour juices into another large bowl. Refrigerate separately, uncovered until cool, then cover and keep chilled overnight.
3. Discard fat from top of chilled juices; reserve juices. Chop pork into ½-inch cubes, discarding excess fat.
4. Thinly slice remaining 2 onions. Heat remaining 3 tablespoons oil in heavy large pot over medium-high heat. Add onions and sauté until soft, stirring often, about 7 minutes. Add remaining 3 tablespoons ancho chile powder, remaining 1½ tablespoons oregano, diced chiles, garlic, and cumin, then stir 30 seconds. Add pork, reserved juices, hominy and red chili sauce. Bring to boil; reduce heat to low.
5. Cover pot with lid slightly ajar and simmer 30 minutes to allow flavors to blend, adding more broth to thin, if desired.
6. Ladle posole into bowls. Garnish with lime wedges, green onion, cilantro, and tortilla shells or chips, cabbage, and radish slices, as desired.

# HOPPIN' JOHN

## DEWBERRY FARM BONUS RECIPE

In Texas, it's traditional to eat black-eyed peas on New Year's Day for good luck, and this old-fashioned recipe is a classic. This is an easy, tasty dish you can toss in the crockpot while you recover from your New Year's Eve festivities. I love it with cornbread to sop up the juices, and maybe a salad on the side if I'm feeling industrious. Collard greens are traditional, and you can pass a bottle of tabasco around the table for those who like a little bit of heat.

INGREDIENTS:

- 1 pound black-eyed peas, soaked overnight in cold water and drained
- 1 medium yellow onion, diced
- 1 medium red bell pepper, diced
- 1 rib celery, diced
- 1 smoked ham hock
- 32 ounces chicken broth
- 2 whole bay leaves
- 5 cloves garlic, minced

- 1 teaspoon black pepper
- 1 teaspoon smoked paprika

## DIRECTIONS:

1. In a 6-quart or larger crockpot, combine the soaked and drained black-eyed peas, onion, red bell pepper, celery, ham hock, chicken stock, bay leaves, garlic, black pepper, and smoked paprika.
2. Cover and cook on low for 7 to 8 hours or on high for 4 to 5 hours, until the beans are tender.
3. Discard the ham hock and bay leaves.
4. Serve with hot rice or cornbread (see recipe for Sweet Texas Cornbread in Breads and Rolls).

# EASY CHICKEN OR TURKEY ENCHILADAS VERDE

## DEWBERRY FARM BONUS RECIPE

INGREDIENTS:

- 2 1/2 cups Verde Sauce (see recipe in sauces) or other green enchilada sauce, preferably tomatillo-based
- 1 1/4 cups crema or sour cream
- 2 cups shredded roasted chicken or turkey
- 1 4-oz. can diced Hatch green chiles (optional)
- 1-2 cups Monterrey Jack cheese
- 1 tablespoon finely chopped yellow onion
- 1/4 teaspoon kosher salt
- 1/4 cup vegetable oil
- 12 corn tortillas

DIRECTIONS:

1. Warm the tomatillo sauce in a small saucepan over low heat. Add 1 cup of the crema or sour cream and heat without letting it boil. Remove from heat and set aside.

2. In a separate saucepan over low heat, warm the chicken or turkey (add a few teaspoons of water or broth if it looks dry; you can also add the small can of Hatch green chiles at this point if you're feeling adventurous). Add the remaining 1/4 cup crema or sour cream, onion, and salt and stir to combine. Remove from heat, cover, and set aside.
3. Line a baking sheet with paper towels. Heat the oil in a small skillet over medium-high heat. When the oil is hot, add a tortilla and let it soften for a few seconds, then flip it and soften the other side and remove the tortilla to the paper-towel-lined baking sheet to drain. Repeat with the remaining tortillas.
4. Heat the oven to 350°F. Pour 1 cup of Verde sauce on a plate, put a warmed tortilla in the sauce and immediately flip it over. Arrange 2 tablespoons of the chicken mixture in a stripe down the center of the tortilla, roll it up, and transfer to a baking dish. Continue with the remaining tortillas, adding additional sauce to the plate when necessary.
5. Pour the remaining sauce over the rolled enchiladas in the baking dish, covering the ends of the tortillas so they don't dry out in the oven. Sprinkle cheese on top, then cover the dish with foil and transfer to the oven, and bake until the enchiladas are heated through and cheese has melted, 15-20 minutes. Serve immediately.

# ALFIE'S SMOKED PORK RIBS

## DYEING SEASON, BOOK 5

INGREDIENTS:

- 6 pounds pork spareribs
- 1 1/2 cups white sugar
- 1/4 cup salt
- 2 1/2 tablespoons ground black pepper
- 3 tablespoons sweet paprika
- 1 teaspoon cayenne pepper, or to taste
- 2 tablespoons garlic powder
- 5 tablespoons pan drippings
- 1/2 cup chopped onion
- 4 cups ketchup
- 3 cups hot water
- 4 tablespoons brown sugar
- cayenne pepper to taste
- salt and pepper to taste
- 1 cup wood chips, soaked

## DIRECTIONS:

1. Clean the ribs, trimming away any excess fat. In a medium bowl, stir together the white sugar, 1/4 cup salt, ground black pepper, paprika, 1 teaspoon cayenne pepper, and garlic powder. Coat ribs liberally with spice mix and place the ribs in two 10x15 inch roasting pans lined with foil, piling two racks of ribs per pan. Cover and refrigerate for at least 8 hours.
2. Preheat oven to 275 degrees and bake uncovered for 3 to 4 hours, or until the ribs are tender and nearly fall apart.
3. Remove 5 tablespoons of drippings from the bottom of the roasting pans and place in a skillet over medium heat. Saute onion in pan drippings until lightly browned and tender. Stir in ketchup and heat for 3 to 4 more minutes, stirring constantly, then mix in water and brown sugar. Season to taste with cayenne pepper, salt, and pepper. Reduce heat to low, cover, and simmer for 1 hour, adding water as necessary to achieve desired thickness.
4. While sauce is cooking, preheat grill for medium-low heat.
5. When ribs are ready to grill, add soaked wood chips to the coals or to the smoker box of a gas grill (I put soaked chips in a "bowl" made of aluminum foil and place it on the burner beneath the grate). Lightly oil grill grate. Place ribs on the grill two racks at a time, making sure not to crowd them. Cook for 20 minutes, turning occasionally.
6. Baste ribs with sauce during the last 10 minutes of grilling to prevent sauce from burning.

# CHICKEN AND DUMPLINGS, SOUTHERN STYLE

## DEWBERRY FARM BONUS RECIPE

My family is originally from the Northeast, so I grew up with fluffy, biscuit-style drop dumplings, but this recipe features southern-style dumplings, which are more like chewy noodles, but absolutely delicious. Although it's not strictly traditional, I sometimes like to leave the celery, carrots, and onion in the broth.

If you're not cooking the chicken yourself, you can always use leftover chicken and turkey, a rotisserie chicken, and store-bought chicken broth (or any you have on hand in the freezer).

INGREDIENTS:

*Chicken and Broth*

- 1 whole chicken, giblets removed
- 2 carrots, cut in 2-inch lengths
- 2 celery stalks, cut in 2-inch lengths
- 1 onion, quartered
- 1 small bunch parsley, tied together with kitchen twine

*Dumplings*

- 1 cup all-purpose flour
- 1 teaspoon salt
- 2 heaping tablespoons vegetable shortening
- 1/2 cup hot water
- 1/2 cup plus 2 tablespoons all-purpose flour

*Soup*

- 2 large chicken bouillon cubes
- 1 tablespoon butter
- 1/4 cup water
- 2 tablespoons flour
- Salt and pepper to taste

DIRECTIONS:

1. Put the chicken, carrots, celery, onion, and parsley in a large stockpot and cover with water. Bring to a quick boil, then cook for one hour. When done, remove chicken to a bowl to cool and strain broth. Return broth to stockpot.
2. Once the chicken is cool, remove the skin and cut or tear the chicken into bite-sized pieces. (You can use all the chicken, or reserve half for another meal, depending on how much chicken you like.)
3. Add the chicken pieces back into the chicken broth, heat to boiling, then add bouillon cubes. Salt and pepper to taste.
4. While chicken broth is coming to a boil, make the dumplings. In a large bowl, using a pastry blender or two knives, cut the shortening and salt into one cup of flour until the shortening is the size of small peas. Add 1/2 cup of hot water and the flour to the mixture. Stir and work the mixture until a soft dough ball forms (firm enough to roll out). Divide the dough into 3 equal-size balls and let the dough rest for 10 minutes.

5. Flour a clean countertop or wood board. Roll each dough ball out one at a time, sprinkling dough with flour as needed to keep it from sticking to the work surface. Roll dough out to about the size of a large pie crust (it will be thin), then cut the dough into strips about an inch wide. Repeat process for the remaining dough balls.
6. Drop dumplings a couple at a time into hot boiling chicken/broth mixture until all have been added to pot, then add butter and continue cooking.
7. Make a slurry by mixing 1/4 cup water and 2 tablespoons flour. Add to soup pot and stir well to thicken the broth, then cook an additional 10 minutes on high until dumplings are cooked. Add salt and pepper to taste.

# SIDE DISHES

# GERMAN POTATO SALAD

## DYEING SEASON, BOOK 5

INGREDIENTS:

- 3 cups diced red, Yukon Gold, or new potatoes (peeling optional)
- 4 slices bacon
- 1 small onion, diced
- 1/4 cup apple cider or white vinegar
- 2 tablespoons water
- 3 tablespoons white sugar
- 1 teaspoon salt
- 1/8 teaspoon ground black pepper
- 1 tablespoon chopped fresh parsley

DIRECTIONS:

1. Place the potatoes into a pot, and fill with enough water to cover. Bring to a boil, and cook for about 10 minutes, or until easily pierced with a fork. Drain, and set aside to cool.

2. Put the bacon in a cold skillet, then turn to medium-high heat. Fry until browned and crisp, turning as needed. Remove bacon from the pan and set aside.
3. Add onion to the bacon grease, and cook over medium heat until browned. Add the vinegar, water, sugar, salt and pepper to the pan. Bring to a boil, then add the potatoes and parsley. Crumble in half of the bacon. Heat through, transfer to a serving dish, and crumble the remaining bacon over the top. Serve warm.

# TEXAS CAVIAR

## DEWBERRY FARM BONUS RECIPE

INGREDIENTS:

- 1 (15 ounce) can black beans, drained and rinsed
- 1 (15 ounce) can black-eyed peas, drained and rinsed
- 1/2 onion, chopped
- 1 pint cherry tomatoes, halved
- 1 bunch green onions, chopped
- 1 green bell pepper, chopped
- 2 jalapeno peppers, chopped
- 1 tablespoon minced garlic
- 1 (8 ounce) bottle Italian dressing
- 1/2 teaspoon ground coriander
- 1 bunch chopped fresh cilantro

DIRECTIONS:

1. Mix all of the ingredients (except for the cilantro) in a large bowl.

2. Cover and chill in the refrigerator at least 2 hours; toss with fresh cilantro to serve.

# BREADS AND ROLLS

# QUINN'S FAMOUS GLAZED MAPLE TWISTS

## KILLER JAM, BOOK 1

INGREDIENTS:

*Dough:*

- 2 3/4 to 3 cups all-purpose flour, divided
- 3/4 cup milk
- 1/4 cup butter
- 3 tablespoons sugar
- 1/2 teaspoon salt
- 1 tablespoon yeast
- 1 teaspoon maple extract
- 1 egg

*Streusel:*

- 1/4 cup melted butter
- 1/2 cup white sugar
- 1/3 cup chopped walnuts
- 1 teaspoon cinnamon
- 1 teaspoon maple extract

*Glaze:*

- 1 cup powdered sugar
- 2 tablespoons melted butter
- 1 to 2 tablespoons milk
- 1/2 teaspoon maple extract
- 1/2 teaspoon vanilla extract

DIRECTIONS:

1. Heat milk and butter until very warm. Blend in a stand mixer with 1 cup of flour, sugar, salt, yeast, egg and maple extract. Beat on low for 2 minutes, then add the rest of the flour, 1/2 cup at a time (you may not need all 3 cups). Knead into a soft dough until smooth and elastic, about five minutes. Cover bowl with plastic wrap and let it rise for 45 minutes or doubled in size. While dough is rising, combine streusel ingredients and set aside.
2. After the dough has risen, divide it into three pieces and roll each piece into a 12" circle. Place the first circle on a buttered 14" pizza pan (or large cookie sheet) covered with parchment paper. Top the first circle with 1/3 of the streusel mixture and spread it in a thin layer; repeat with second and third pieces.
3. Find a glass that is 2" across and center it on each circle(press down a little to make a mark). Using scissors, cut from the outer edge into the cup mark, making 16 wedges.
4. Gently lift and twist each wedge 5 times, tucking in the ends so that they stay twisted, and arrange on the pan.
5. Lightly cover the dough with plastic wrap and let it rise for about 45 minutes to an hour. Bake in a 375° oven for 20-25 minutes. While twists are baking, whisk together glaze

ingredients. Remove twists from oven and let rest for 5 minutes, then drizzle glaze over twists.

## QUINN'S VANOCKA (CZECH CHRISTMAS BREAD)

### FATAL FROST, BOOK 2

INGREDIENTS:

- 1 package of yeast
- 1/4 cup warm water
- 1/2 cup sugar
- 1/4 cup butter
- 2 teaspoons salt
- 2 eggs
- 5 1/2 - 6 cups all-purpose flour
- 1 cup warm milk
- 1 teaspoon lemon zest
- 1/4 teaspoon mace
- 1 cup light raisins
- 1/2 cup nuts (Quinn likes pecans), chopped
- 1 egg yolk, beaten

DIRECTIONS:

1. Dissolve yeast in warm water. While yeast is dissolving, cream sugar, butter, and salt in a large bowl. Beat in eggs, then one cup of flour. When the mixture is smooth, beat in milk, lemon peel, mace, and the yeast mixture, then stir in as much flour as you can with a spoon (you'll add the rest later). Stir in raisins and nuts and turn dough out onto a floured board.
2. Knead in enough of the remaining flour to make a fairly soft dough that is smooth and elastic: this should take 3 to 5 minutes. Place the dough in a lightly greased bowl, turning once to grease the entire surface of the dough, then cover, let rise in warm place until doubled.
3. When dough is ready, divide the dough into two equal sections. Divide one section of the dough into fourths (this will be the bottom braid): cover and let rest 10 minutes. While the first section is resting, divide the remaining dough into 5 sections, then cover and set it aside.
4. On a lightly floured surface, form each of the first 4 sections into 16-inch long ropes. On a greased baking sheet, arrange the four ropes, 1 inch apart. Beginning in the middle of the ropes, braid the dough ropes toward each end (you'll braid first one half of the ropes, and then the other). To braid the four ropes, overlap the center 2 ropes to form an X, then take the outside left rope and cross over the closest middle rope. Then, take the outside right rope and cross it under the closest middle rope. Repeat braiding until you reach the end, then pinch the ends together and tuck them under. Turn the baking sheet and repeat the process to braid the opposite end. When the dough is braided, gently pull width of braid out slightly. Then, on a separate pan or board, form the remaining 5 sections into 16-inch long ropes. Braid 3 of the ropes together, then brush the 4-strand braid with

water and center the second braid on top; gently pull the width of top braid out. Twist the remaining two ropes of dough together and brush the top braid with water, then place the twist on top of the second braid.
5. Cover the shaped dough and let rise till nearly double. While dough is rising, preheat oven to 350°F. When dough has almost doubled, brush surface of the shaped dough with egg yolk and bake in oven for 35-40 minutes.

# QUINN'S BLUE ONION MAZANEC

## DYEING SEASON, BOOK 5

INGREDIENTS:

- 1 package instant dry yeast
- 10 fl oz lukewarm milk
- 4 cups all-purpose flour
- 3/4 cup granulated sugar
- 6 1/2 tbs unsalted butter, softened
- 1/2 tsp salt
- 1 tsp pure vanilla extract
- 1/4 cup raisins
- 1/4 cup sliced almonds
- 1 egg plus one egg yolk
- 1 tbs water

DIRECTIONS:

1. Mix the package of yeast with the lukewarm milk in a small bowl. Add a pinch of sugar and stir gently, then cover with a

kitchen towel and let stand until the mixture is frothy (about 5 minutes). While yeast is proving, soak raisins in boiling water until plump, then drain and set aside.

2. Cream together softened butter and sugar with an electric mixer. Add in egg yolk, salt and vanilla extract, then mix until mixture is smooth and creamy. Add yeast mixture and mix again. Add flour in three portions until completely combined. Add raisins and mix with the dough hook attachment for about a minute, until a soft dough forms. Place the dough in a large, greased bowl, cover with plastic wrap sprayed with cooking spray and let rise in a warm spot for at least an hour, or until it has doubled in size.

3. Once the dough has risen, remove from the bowl and shape it into a ball, smoothing out the surface. Place dough on a baking sheet lined with parchment paper and cover with a kitchen towel. While dough is rising, preheat oven to 350 and whisk an egg with about a tablespoon of water in a small bowl. When dough has risen (about a half hour), remove towel and brush loaf with the egg wash, then sprinkle generously with the sliced almonds. Bake for 45 – 55 minutes, until the loaf is golden brown and sounds hollow when tapped on bottom. If the loaf begins to brown too quickly, cover with foil to prevent it from burning.

4. Let cool, then slice and spread with butter and your favorite jam.

## SWEET TEXAS CORNBREAD

### DEWBERRY FARM BONUS RECIPE

Wonderful with Hoppin' John on a cold winter day. Or just butter. Lots and lots of butter. And a touch of honey if you're feeling decadent.

INGREDIENTS:

- 1 cup flour
- 1 cup yellow cornmeal
- 1/2 cup sugar (more or less, depending on how sweet you like it — you can taste the batter)
- 1 teaspoon. salt
- 2 teaspoons baking powder
- 2 eggs
- 1 cup milk
- 1/3 c. plus 2 teaspoons vegetable oil
- 1 teaspoon vanilla

DIRECTIONS:

1. Preheat the oven to 400 degrees. In a small bowl, without stirring, soak cornmeal in milk for 15 minutes. Spray a 10-inch round oven-proof skillet or pan (cast iron is ideal).
2. In a large bowl, combine the flour, sugar, salt and baking powder with a whisk. Stir in eggs, cornmeal and milk mixture, vegetable oil, and vanilla, mixing until just combined. (Batter will be slightly lumpy.) Pour batter into prepared pan and bake for 20-25 minutes, or until a toothpick inserted into center of the cornbread comes out clean.

# DESSERTS

# BUTTERCUP PECAN PIE

## DYEING SEASON, BOOK 5

A classic Texas dessert. I love, love, love pecan pie, but if I make it, I end up eating the whole thing.

INGREDIENTS:

- 1 unbaked pie crust (store-bought or homemade, recipe follows)
- 3 eggs, beaten
- 3/4 cup sugar
- 3/4 cup white corn syrup
- 3 tbsp melted butter
- 1 tsp vanilla
- 1 tsp white vinegar
- 1/8 tsp salt
- 1 cup chopped pecans

## DIRECTIONS:

1. Mix all ingredients thoroughly, except the pecans. Add the pecans and pour in the mixture into an unbaked pie shell. (You can use a store-bought one or make one: recipe follows.)
2. Preheat oven to 375 and bake for 25-30 minutes. Testing for doneness with a knife inserted in the center. Pie is done when knife comes out clean.

*Pie Crust (makes one two-crust or two one-crust pie shells)*

## INGREDIENTS:

- 2 cups flour
- 1 tsp salt
- 2/3 cup plus 2 tbsp shortening
- 4-5 tbsp ice-cold water

## DIRECTIONS:

1. In a medium size bowl, combine the flour and salt, then cut in shortening with a pastry blender or two forks.
2. Sprinkle water 1 tbsp at a time until all flour is moistened, taking care not to overwork.
3. Shape into a ball and roll out on floured surface.

# TEXAS PEACH COBBLER

## DEWBERRY FARM BONUS RECIPE

This is wonderful on its own, but even better with a big scoop of vanilla ice cream!

INGREDIENTS:

*Filling*

- 4 cups peaches (frozen, or ripe, sliced and peeled)
- 1/2 teaspoon vanilla
- 1 tablespoon lemon juice
- 4 tablespoons sugar

*Batter*

- 1 1/4 cups all-purpose flour
- 6 tablespoons melted butter
- 3/4 cup sugar
- 2 tablespoons baking powder
- 1/2 teaspoon salt
- 1 teaspoon cinnamon

- 1 cup milk
- 1 teaspoon vanilla
- 1 tablespoon turbinado sugar

DIRECTIONS:

1. Preheat oven to 350 degrees, and peel the peaches if using fresh. (To peel fresh peaches, blanch them in boiling water briefly; this will make peeling a cinch.)
2. Combine the peaches with sugar, lemon juice & vanilla and set aside.
3. Pour melted butter into an 8-inch square baking dish, making sure it covers the bottom.
4. Combine flour, sugar, baking powder, salt, and cinnamon in a medium bowl. In a separate small bowl, mix milk and 1/2 tsp. vanilla together. Add milk mixture to flour mixture, stirring just until moist. Spoon batter mixture over butter and spread evenly.
5. Spoon the peach mixture over the batter, gently pressing the peaches into the batter.
6. Bake for 40 minutes, sprinkle with turbinado sugar, then bake for an additional 10 minutes or until the crust is golden.

# BIENENSTICH (BEE STING CAKE)

## WICKED HARVEST, BOOK 6

I first had this cake in Munich, and I've loved it ever since. So does Lucy, oddly enough. :)

INGREDIENTS:

*Cake*

- 1 3/4 cup flour
- 2 Tbsp sugar
- 2 1/4 tsp yeast (1 packet)
- pinch of salt
- 1 egg (at room temperature)
- 1/4 cup melted butter
- 1/3 cup milk (at room temperature)

*Topping*

- 1/4 cup butter
- 1 Tbsp honey
- 6 Tbsp sugar

- 1 1/2 Tbsp heavy whipping cream
- 3/4 cup sliced almonds

*Filling*

- 2 cups heavy whipping cream
- 1 3.4-oz. packet vanilla pudding mix

DIRECTIONS:

1. Combine the flour, sugar, yeast, salt, butter, egg, and milk in a large bowl, kneading the dough a few times until it becomes smooth.
2. Remove the dough from the bowl and spray the bowl with cooking spray, then return the dough to the bowl. Cover with a towel and let it rise for 30 minutes.
3. While the cake dough is rising, make the topping by melting the butter, honey, and sugar in a small saucepan over medium heat. When the butter has melted, add the cream and stir until the sugar is dissolved. Remove the saucepan from heat and stir in sliced almonds.
4. Preheat the oven to 350. Spray or grease an 8×8 baking dish and then place a sheet of parchment paper in the dish so that the edges hang over the sides. Roll out the dough and press it into the dish, then prick the dough several times with a fork. Pour the almond topping onto dough, spreading it out evenly. Bake the cake for 35 minutes; the topping will be golden brown when the cake is done.
5. Let the cake cool for a few minutes and use the parchment paper to remove it from the baking dish. When you can touch the topping with your fingers, use a long serrated knife to cut the cake in two layers.
6. Place the top layer on a sheet of parchment paper and use the same knife to cut the top layer into nine equal-sized

pieces. (It's much easier to cut the top layer when it's still a bit warm.)
7. Add the pudding powder to the heavy cream and whip to stiff peaks, then spread the filling over the bottom cake layer. Gently place the top layer onto the cream filling piece by piece. Chill the cake for 1 hour or until the filling is set.
8. When you're ready to serve the cake, slice the Bienenstich gently with a sharp knife while you hold the top lightly, being careful not to not to use too much pressure (or else the filling will spill out). Guten Appetit!

# GOAT MILK FLAN

## WICKED HARVEST, BOOK 6

INGREDIENTS:

- Nonstick cooking spray
- 1/3 cup granulated sugar
- 2 cups goat's milk (you can use cow's milk instead, if you're not a fan of goat's milk)
- 1/2 cup plus 1 tablespoon superfine sugar
- 3 egg yolks, beaten
- 2 whole eggs, beaten
- 1/4 teaspoon vanilla extract

DIRECTIONS:

1. Preheat oven to 350 degrees and lightly grease four 6-ounce ramekins with nonstick cooking spray.
2. Add the granulated sugar to a small saucepan set over high heat and let the sugar melt without stirring. As it melts, gently swirl the pan around to make sure it melts evenly.

When the sugar has turned to caramel and is dark amber in color, carefully divide the caramel evenly among the ramekins. (If your caramel isn't working and you want an easier approach, you can simply pour a tablespoon or two of dark corn syrup into the bottom of each ramekin).

3. Add the milk and the superfine sugar to a saucepan and bring the mixture to a gentle simmer. As the milk heats, add the egg yolks, whole eggs and vanilla to a large mixing bowl, whisking together until foamy. Add a little of the hot milk to temper the eggs, stirring to combine, then gradually add the rest of the milk so it doesn't cook the eggs. Once the milk is completely incorporated, stir the mixture well and then divide it evenly among the four ramekins.
4. Line a deep baking dish or roasting pan with a kitchen towel and carefully place the ramekins on top. Place the dish in the oven, then fill it with hot water so it comes 3/4 of the way up the sides of the ramekins.
5. Bake until the custards are set, about 35 minutes, and remove the ramekins from the oven and allow to cool. (I often use tongs or potholders to take them out of the roasting pan and cool them on a wire rack; they can be slippery, though, so be careful.) Chill flans in the fridge before inverting onto a plate to serve.

# FRESH STRAWBERRY CUSTARD PIE

## KILLER JAM, BOOK 1

INGREDIENTS:

- 3 cups sliced strawberries
- 1 cup white sugar
- 2 tablespoons butter
- 1 egg
- 2 tablespoons flour
- 1 unbaked pie shell (see Pecan Pie recipe for pie shell recipe)
- 2 tablespoons brown sugar
- 3 tablespoons flour
- 2 tablespoons butter

DIRECTIONS:

1. Preheat oven to 375. In a mixer, combine 1 cup of sugar, egg, 2 tablespoons of butter and 2 tablespoons of flour until smooth. Fold strawberries into the batter, and pour into uncooked pie shell.

2. In a second bowl, mix brown sugar, remaining 3 tablespoons of flour, and remaining 2 tablespoons of butter. Mix with a fork and sprinkle over the unbaked pie. Bake 50 minutes or until set (cover the crust with strips of foil it it browns too quickly).
3. Serve warm or cold, with whipped cream if desired.

# GRANDMA VOGEL'S LEBKUCHEN BARS

## FATAL FROST, BOOK 2

INGREDIENTS:

*Dough*

- 1/2 cup roasted hazelnuts
- 1/2 cup almond meal
- 2 3/4 cups sifted all-purpose flour
- 2 tablespoons unsweetened cocoa
- 1 1/2 teaspoons baking powder
- 1/2 teaspoon baking soda
- 2 teaspoons cinnamon
- 1 teaspoon ginger
- 1/2 teaspoon nutmeg
- 1/2 teaspoon cloves
- 1/2 teaspoon allspice
- 1/4 teaspoon cardamom
- 1/2 teaspoon salt
- 1/2 cup tightly packed chopped candied orange rind
- 1/4 cup tightly packed chopped crystallized ginger
- 4 tablespoons unsalted butter

- 3/4 cup dark brown sugar
- 1 cup honey
- 2 large eggs
- 1 tablespoon pure vanilla extract

*Glaze*

- 3 cups confectioners' sugar
- 1 tablespoon kirsch, rum, or vanilla extract
- 3 to 4 tablespoons warm water

DIRECTIONS:

1. Combine hazelnuts, almond meal, flour, cocoa, baking powder, baking soda, cinnamon, powdered ginger, nutmeg, cloves, allspice, cardamom, and salt in a medium sized bowl.
2. Put the candied orange rind and crystallized ginger into a food processor along with 1 cup of the dry ingredient mixture and pulse until very finely chopped. Add the remaining dry ingredients and pulse to combine.
3. In a large bowl, cream butter with brown sugar at medium speed, then add honey and beat until smooth. Beat in eggs and vanilla to combine; then add dry ingredients by the heaping spoonful and beat at a very low speed until combined (a paddle attachment on a standing mixer is ideal for this). Scrape sides and bottom of bowl and beat again until evenly combined.
4. Line a half-sheet pan (13" x 8") with parchment paper, extending paper a few inches over the short sides. Lightly spray the unlined sides of the pan with nonstick cooking spray. Spread the dough into a thin, even layer and bake in the center of the oven about 25 minutes, until surface is dimpled and a toothpick inserted into the center comes out clean. The cake should be springy but firm.

5. Cool on a rack. While the bars are cooling, whisk confectioners' sugar with kirsch, vanilla extract or rum and add enough water to make a thin but spreadable glaze.
6. Spread glaze on just-warm cake and let cool completely. When cool, slide the cake (with parchment) from the pan onto a cutting board and cut into bars. Ideally, leave the lebkuchen in an airtight container at room temperature for at least one day before serving to let the flavors meld. It will keep up to two weeks.

# HALLOWEEN PUMPKIN BARS

## DEADLY BREW, BOOK 3

INGREDIENTS:

- ½ cup butter
- 1 cup brown sugar, packed
- 2 eggs
- 1 tsp vanilla extract
- ½ tsp baking soda
- ½ tsp baking powder
- ½ tsp salt
- 1 tsp cinnamon
- ¼ tsp ginger
- ¼ tsp nutmeg
- 1 cup flour
- ¾ cup pumpkin, canned or cooked
- 3 oz pkg. cream cheese, softened
- 6 tbs butter, softened
- 2 cup confectioners' sugar
- 1 tsp vanilla extract
- 1/2 tsp almond extract

## DIRECTIONS:

*Cake:*

1. Preheat oven to 350 degrees. Cream butter and brown sugar until fluffy, then beat in eggs.
2. Add 1 teaspoon vanilla extract and beat until smooth, then beat in baking soda, baking powder, salt, cinnamon, ginger, and nutmeg.
3. Mix in flour alternately with pumpkin. Do not overmix. Spread in buttered and floured 9" x 13" baking pan and bake for 20-25 minutes.

*Cream cheese frosting:*

1. Beat cream cheese and butter until fluffy.
2. Add confectioners sugar, 1 teaspoon vanilla extract, and 1/2 tsp almond extract. Beat until smooth.
3. Frost cooled pumpkin bars.

# LUCY'S APPLE DUMPLINGS

## DEADLY BREW, BOOK 3

INGREDIENTS:

- Unbaked pastry for double-crust pie (use frozen from the store or your favorite recipe)
- 6 large Granny Smith apples, peeled and cored
- ½ cup butter
- ¾ cup brown sugar
- 1 teaspoon ground cinnamon
- ½ teaspoon ground nutmeg
- 3 cups water
- 2 cups white sugar
- 1 tsp vanilla extract

DIRECTIONS:

1. Preheat oven to 400 degrees and butter a 9x13 inch pan. On a lightly floured surface, roll pastry into a large rectangle, about twenty-four by sixteen inches, and cut into six square

pieces. Place an apple on each pastry square with the cored opening facing upward. Cut butter into eight pieces and place one piece of butter in the opening of each apple, reserving the remaining butter for sauce. Divide the brown sugar between apples, poking some inside each cored opening and the rest around the base of each apple, and sprinkle cinnamon and nutmeg over the apples.
2. With slightly wet fingertips, bring one corner of the pastry square up to the top of the apple, then bring the opposite corner to the top and press together. Bring up the two remaining corners and seal, then slightly pinch the dough at the sides to completely seal in the apple. Repeat with the remaining apples. Place in prepared baking dish.
3. In a saucepan, combine water, white sugar, vanilla extract, and reserved butter. Place over medium heat and bring to a boil in a large saucepan. Boil for five minutes, or until sugar is dissolved, and carefully pour over dumplings.
4. Bake in preheated oven for 50 to 60 minutes. To serve, place each apple dumpling in a bowl and spoon some sauce over the top.

# GRANDMA VOGEL'S SNICKERDOODLES

## MISTLETOE MURDER, BOOK 4

INGREDIENTS:

*Cookies*

- 8 tablespoons (½ cup) unsalted butter, at room temperature*
- ¾ cup sugar
- 1 large egg
- 1 teaspoon vanilla extract
- 1 teaspoon baking powder
- ½ teaspoon salt*
- 1⅓ cups flour

*If you use salted butter, decrease the salt to ¼ teaspoon.

*Coating*

- 2 tablespoons sugar
- 1–1½ teaspoons ground cinnamon, to taste

## DIRECTIONS:

1. Preheat oven to 375°F and lightly grease (or line with parchment) two baking sheets. Beat together the butter and sugar until smooth. Add the egg, beating until smooth, then beat in the vanilla, salt, and baking powder. Add the flour, mixing until totally incorporated.
2. Make the coating by shaking together the sugar and cinnamon in a medium-sized zip-top plastic bag.
3. Drop small (1"-diameter) balls of dough into the bag. Roll or toss the cookies in the cinnamon-sugar until they're completely coated.
4. Space the cookies at least 1½" apart on the prepared baking sheets, and use a flat-bottom glass to flatten them to about ⅜" thick; they'll be about 1½" in diameter.
5. Bake cookies for 8 minutes (for soft cookies) to 10 minutes (for crunchier cookies). Remove from the oven and cool them on the pan until they're firm enough to transfer to a rack to cool completely.

# ALMOND CRESCENT COOKIES

## MISTLETOE MURDER, BOOK 4

INGREDIENTS:

- 1 cup (2 sticks) butter, softened
- ½ cup powdered sugar plus more for rolling cookies
- 2 teaspoons vanilla extract
- 1 teaspoon almond extract
- 2 cups all-purpose flour
- ¼ teaspoon salt (not needed if your butter is salted)
- 1 cup finely chopped or ground almonds

DIRECTIONS:

1. Preheat oven to 325 degrees F. In a mixing bowl, cream butter, powdered sugar, vanilla extract, and almond extract. Blend in flour, salt, and nuts until dough holds together.
2. Shape dough into 1-inch balls and place 1-inch apart on baking sheets lined with parchment paper. Bake 15 minutes

and until set, but not brown. Cool slightly, then roll in powdered sugar. Cool completely, then roll again in powdered sugar.

# LEBKUCHEN (GINGERBREAD) OKTOBERFEST HEARTS

## WICKED HARVEST, BOOK 6

INGREDIENTS:

- 3/4 cup softened (not warm) butter
- 1/4 cup brown sugar
- 1 tablespoon ground ginger
- 1 teaspoon ground cinnamon
- 1/4 teaspoon ground nutmeg
- 1/4 teaspoon ground cloves
- 1 teaspoon finely grated lemon zest
- 1/2 teaspoon finely grated orange zest
- 3/4 cup molasses
- 1/3 cup honey
- 2 medium eggs, beaten
- 3 to 4 cups all-purpose flour
- 1 teaspoon baking soda
- 1/4 teaspoon salt
- Egg white for brushing
- Royal Icing for decorating

## DIRECTIONS:

1. Cream butter and sugar in a large bowl until light and fluffy, then add spices and zests, beating until they are incorporated. In a small saucepan over medium-high heat, heat molasses and honey until boiling and allow to cool for 10 minutes. Add the molasses mixture to the creamed butter, stirring constantly, then beat in the eggs one by one and combine thoroughly.
2. Sift 3 cups flour, baking soda and salt together in a large bowl and stir into the butter/molasses mixture one cup at a time, adding as much of the remaining flour as needed to get a soft but not sticky dough. Shape dough into a ball, cover with plastic wrap, and chill overnight.
3. Preheat oven to 350 degrees. Roll out chilled dough to about 1/3-inch thick. Using cutters or working freehand, cut the dough into whatever shapes you have in mind (hearts are typical for Oktoberfest; if you're adding ribbon to the top, as is traditional in Germany, don't forget to add a hole for the ribbon). Brush cookies with lightly beaten egg white, place on a parchment-covered baking sheet with plenty of space between the cookies, and bake for 12 to 15 minutes. Try not to let the edges brown!
4. To decorate Oktoberfest Hearts, wait until completely cooled and decorate with a piped stiff royal icing, made from a mixture of slightly beaten egg whites, a little lemon juice and confectioner's (powdered or icing) sugar added gradually until the icing becomes stiff and stands in peaks. You can color some of the icing if you like (blue is traditional), or leave it white. In Germany, words like "I love you" or "Oktoberfest" are frequently piped, along with a decorative border. Have fun!

# CHOCOLATE GLAZED LEBKUCHEN

## WICKED HARVEST, BOOK 6

INGREDIENTS:

*Lebkuchen*

- 1/2 + 1/3 cup dark brown sugar, packed
- 2/3 cup honey
- Scant 1/4 cup butter, softened
- Finely grated zest of 1 orange
- 2 1/2 cups flour
- 1 1/4 cups ground almonds
- 1 tbsp cocoa powder
- 2 1/2 tsp ground ginger
- 1 1/2 tsp ground cinnamon
- 1/2 tsp ground allspice
- 1/4 tsp ground cloves
- 1/4 tsp ground nutmeg
- 1/2 tsp salt
- 1/2 tsp baking powder
- 1/4 tsp baking soda
- 2 medium eggs

*Glaze*

- 1 1/2 cups powdered sugar, sifted
- 2 tbsp water
- 7oz. dark chocolate, chopped

DIRECTIONS:

1. Combine the sugar, honey, butter and orange zest in a large bowl and beat with an electric mixer until smooth. In a separate bowl, sift together the flour, ground almonds, cocoa powder, spices, salt, baking powder and baking soda and set aside.
2. Add the eggs to the sugar mixture one at a time, beating well after each addition, then add the flour mixture to the sugar mixture a cup at a time, mixing until well combined.
3. When the dough is mixed, cover the bowl and place in the fridge for half an hour (preferably overnight).
4. Preheat the oven to 350 degrees and line two baking sheets with parchment paper. Scoop out balls of dough using a measuring spoon or coffee scoop, about 1 1/2 tbsp at a time, and roll dough balls between slightly damp hands until round and smooth. Place on the baking sheets with ample space between them, flattening them slightly with your fingers.
5. Bake cookies for about 15 minutes; when they are done, they will be firm and lightly browned, and a toothpick inserted into the center will out clean. Transfer the cookies to a wire rack and allow to cool completely.
6. When the cookies are cooled, measure the powdered sugar into a small bowl and gradually mix in enough of the water to form a slightly runny icing (if it is too wet it will run off the cookies). Place a wire rack on a baking sheet.
7. Dip the tops of the cookies into the glaze, allow the excess

to drip off, and then place them right-side up on the wire rack to set.

8. Once the sugar glaze has set, melt the chocolate, either in a double boiler or in short bursts in the microwave (check it often), then pour it into a small bowl. Line a baking sheet with parchment paper. Dip the bottoms of the cookies into the chocolate, allowing the excess to drip off, then place the cookies chocolate-side-down on the parchment paper to set. Once the glaze is set, store the cookies in an airtight container.

# CANDIES

# TEXAS PECAN PRALINES

## SLAY BELLS RING, A DEWBERRY FARMS CHRISTMAS STORY

The classic Texas confection. Yum.

INGREDIENTS:

- 1 cup brown sugar
- ⅓ cup heavy whipping cream
- ¼ cup salted butter (half a stick)
- 1 teaspoon pure vanilla extract
- 1 cup powdered sugar
- 1 1/2 cups pecan halves (or chopped pecans)

DIRECTIONS:

1. Line two large cookie sheets with parchment paper.
2. Put the brown sugar, whipping cream, butter, and vanilla in a medium saucepan and bring to a boil over medium heat, stirring constantly. Boil for about one minute, then remove

saucepan from heat. Immediately whisk in the powdered sugar, then gently stir in the pecans.
3. Allow the mixture to thicken and cool slightly (about a minute or two).
4. Drop heaping spoonfuls of the praline mixture onto paper, and allow candy to set and cool for at least 30 minutes. You can accelerate the process by putting the cookie sheets into the refrigerator.

## BROWN SUGAR FUDGE BALLS

### FATAL FROST, BOOK 2

INGREDIENTS:

- 2 tablespoons softened unsalted butter
- 2 cups light brown sugar
- 1 cup sugar
- 1 cup half-and-half
- 1 pinch salt
- 1 teaspoon vanilla extract
- 1 cup chopped pecans
- 32 ounces bittersweet chocolate or 32 ounces semisweet chocolate, chopped
- 3/4 cup chocolate sprinkles or finely chopped pecans

DIRECTIONS:

1. Coat inside of medium metal bowl with 1/2 teaspoon butter, then place remaining butter in the same bowl and set aside.

2. In a medium saucepan, combine sugars, half and half and salt. Stir over medium-low heat until sugars are almost dissolved, frequently brushing down sides of pan with a wet pastry brush (to capture sugar crystals), about 12 - 15 minutes. Increase heat to medium and continue to stir until it comes to boil, occasionally brushing down sides of pan (about 10 minutes). Attach candy thermometer and boil syrup without stirring until candy thermometer registers 234°F, about 16 minutes (caramel will bubble vigorously in pan).
3. Move the thermometer to the bowl with the butter and pour caramel over butter (do not scrape pan). Add vanilla, but do not stir. Cool caramel to 112°F (about 1 hour 30 minutes).
4. Using an electric mixer, beat caramel until sheen just begins to disappear and mixture thickens slightly, about 4 minutes. Stir in chopped pecans. Cool mixture until thick enough to roll into balls (about 2 hours).
5. When mixture is cool, line 4 baking sheets with waxed paper. Using about 1 tablespoon mixture for each ball, spoon mixture in 48 mounds on 1 sheet. Press or roll each mound between palms of hands into a ball, then refrigerate 30 minutes.
6. When balls are cool, stir chocolate in medium bowl set over saucepan of barely simmering water until smooth and candy thermometer registers 115°F (do not allow bottom of bowl to touch water). Remove bowl from saucepan and drop 1 ball into chocolate, using a fork to turn it and coat all sides. When ball is coated, lift ball from chocolate, allowing excess to drip into bowl, and slide ball off fork onto second waxed-paper covered sheet. Repeat with 15 balls, rewarming chocolate as needed to maintain temperature of 115°F. While chocolate is still wet, sprinkle with 1/4 cup sprinkles or chopped pecans.
7. Repeat with remaining fudge balls and sprinkles/nuts in 2

more batches, placing 16 balls on each of remaining 2 unused sheets. Chill balls until coating is firm, about 30 minutes.
8. Can be made 2 weeks ahead. Refrigerate in covered containers and let stand 20 minutes at room temperature before serving.

# CARAMEL TURTLES

## SLAY BELLS RING, A DEWBERRY FARMS CHRISTMAS STORY

INGREDIENTS:

- 1 teaspoon plus 1 cup butter, divided
- 1 cup light corn syrup
- 2-1/4 cups packed brown sugar
- 1/8 teaspoon salt
- 1 can (14 ounces) sweetened condensed milk
- 1 teaspoon vanilla extract
- 1-1/2 pounds pecan halves, toasted
- 3/4 cup milk chocolate chips
- 3/4 cup semisweet chocolate chips
- 4 teaspoons shortening

DIRECTIONS:

1. Line baking sheets with parchment or waxed paper; lightly coat with cooking spray and set aside. Butter the sides of a heavy saucepan with 1 teaspoon butter. Cube remaining

butter and place in the saucepan; then add the corn syrup, brown sugar, and salt. Cook and stir until sugar is melted.
2. Gradually stir in milk. Cook and stir over medium heat until mixture comes to a boil, then cook and stir until a candy thermometer reads 248° (firm-ball stage), or about 15-16 minutes. Remove from the heat and stir in vanilla, then gently stir in pecans. Drop by rounded teaspoonfuls onto prepared baking sheets and refrigerate until firm, about 10-15 minutes.
3. When caramel has firmed up, melt chips and shortening in the microwave in short bursts or in a double boiler on low heat; stir until smooth. Drizzle over clusters and chill until firm.
4. Store turtles in the refrigerator.

# CANDY CANE FUDGE

## MISTLETOE MURDER, BOOK 4

**INGREDIENTS:**

- 2 (10-ounce) packages vanilla baking chips OR semisweet baking chips
- 1 (14-ounce) can sweetened condensed milk
- ½ teaspoon peppermint extract
- 1½ cups crushed candy canes
- 1 dash red or green food coloring (if using white chocolate… this is optional)

**DIRECTIONS:**

1. Line an 8-inch square baking pan with aluminum foil, and grease the foil.
2. Combine the vanilla chips and sweetened condensed milk in a saucepan over medium heat. Stir frequently until almost melted, remove from heat, and continue to stir until

smooth. When chips are completely melted, stir in the peppermint extract, food coloring, and candy canes.
3. Spread evenly in the bottom of the prepared pan. Chill for 2 hours, then cut into squares.

## BUTTERSCOTCH SQUARES

### SLAY BELLS RING, A DEWBERRY FARMS CHRISTMAS STORY

INGREDIENTS:

- 2 cups light brown sugar
- 3/4 cup heavy whipping cream
- 6 tablespoons butter
- 1/2 teaspoon vanilla
- 1/4 teaspoon salt
- 1 cup powdered sugar
- 16 ounces melting chocolate for dipping (dark or milk, your choice)

DIRECTIONS:

1. Line a 9x9" pan with foil and spray with cooking spray.
2. Add brown sugar, cream, and butter to a saucepan over medium-high heat and stir until melted. Bring mixture to a rolling boil, reduce heat to low, and put a candy thermometer into the pot

3. Stir mixture occasionally and simmer until the mixture reaches 236º (about 7 or 8 minutes).
4. Turn off heat and whisk in vanilla and salt, then whisk in powdered sugar until well combined. Pour mixture into prepared pan. Allow to set at room temperature for a few hours.
5. When candy is set and ready to cut, turn it out from the pan onto a cutting board. With a large kitchen knife, using small, swift cuts so as not to break or flake the candy, cut the square into quarters, then divide the quarters into smaller squares.
6. Melt the chocolate according to directions on the package. Using your fingers or a toothpick, dip each candy square into the melted chocolate, tapping off excess.
7. Put finished candy on a wax-paper- or parchment- lined cookie sheet and chill to set.

# BEVERAGES

# BUBBA ALLEN'S GLÜHWEIN (MULLED WINE)

## FATAL FROST, BOOK 2

I first had this at a market stall on a cold winter day in Koblenz, Germany, and the hot, spiced wine was a perfect warm-up for this chilled Texas girl. "Glühwein" means "glow wine" in German, and this will make your insides glow for sure!

INGREDIENTS:

- 1 (750 ml) bottle of dry red wine
- 1 orange, sliced into rounds
- 1/4 cup brandy (optional)
- 1/4 cup honey or sugar
- 8 whole cloves
- 2 cinnamon sticks
- 2 star anise
- 3 cardamom pods
- optional garnish: citrus slices (orange, lemon and/or lime), extra cinnamon sticks, or extra star anise

## DIRECTIONS:

1. Combine all ingredients in a non-aluminum saucepan, and bring to a simmer (not a boil) over medium-high heat.
2. Reduce heat to medium-low, and let the wine simmer for at least 15 minutes or up to 3 hours.
3. Pour wine through a strainer and serve warm with garnishes as desired.

# TEXAS SWEET TEA

If you order tea at a restaurant in Texas, you will invariably be served a big glass of refreshing iced tea. (If you don't want it iced, you have to specifically ask for "hot tea.") Sweet tea is almost always on offer, and is a classic Texas cooler in the summer. Here's how to make a batch at home, no matter where you live.

INGREDIENTS:

- 1 ounce loose tea leaves
- ice cubes
- 1 1/8 cup granulated sugar
- lemon slices for garnish

DIRECTIONS:

1. Boil half a gallon of filtered water in a large pot. When the water starts bubbling, remove pot from heat, add tea leaves,

and agitate the water for 30 seconds. Steep for 4 1/2 minutes.
2. While the tea is steeping, fill a gallon-size pitcher with ice cubes (ice halts the steeping process). Pour the sugar over the ice cubes.
3. Place a fine wire mesh sieve over the pitcher's opening to catch the tea leaves.
4. Pour the brewed tea through the sieve. The hot liquid will melt the ice and begin to dissolve the sugar.
5. Discard the leaves and stir until all the sugar is incorporated. (Don't be alarmed if the tea gets cloudy, as this will sometimes happens.)
6. Refrigerate until cool, and serve in a tall glass with ice and lemon slices for garnish.

# MULLED HONEY WINE

## DEADLY BREW, BOOK 3

INGREDIENTS:

- 2 cinnamon sticks
- 5 whole allspice
- 5 black peppercorns
- 5 cardamom seeds
- 7 whole cloves
- 3 one-inch pieces of candied or fresh ginger
- 1 orange, sliced
- 2 liters mead (I like Blessed Bee)
- Honey to taste
- Amaretto (optional, but recommended)
- 6 inch square of cheesecloth
- Kitchen twine

DIRECTIONS:

1. Wrap the spices in a piece of cheesecloth and secure it with

twine to make a spice bag. Combine the mead, the spice bag, and the orange slices in a pot and bring to a boil, then reduce heat to a simmer. Let the mead and spices simmer for at least 30 minutes, then discard the orange and spice bag and add honey to taste.
2. Serve hot in a glass (with an optional shot of amaretto). If desired, garnish with an orange twist or a cinnamon stick.

# THE HITCHING POST'S TOM & JERRYS

## MISTLETOE MURDER, BOOK 4

INGREDIENTS:

- 3 eggs, separated
- 3 tablespoons powdered sugar
- ½ teaspoon ground allspice
- ½ teaspoon ground cinnamon
- ½ teaspoon ground cloves
- 4 ounces brandy, lukewarm
- 3 cups hot milk
- Freshly grated nutmeg

DIRECTIONS:

1. In a large, clean bowl, beat the egg whites until stiff peaks form.
2. In a separate bowl, beat the egg yolks until light in color, then gradually beat in the sugar, allspice, cinnamon, and cloves.

3. When thoroughly mixed, fold the yolk mixture into the whites.
4. Pour 2 tablespoons into four mugs each. Add 1 ounce brandy and 1 ounce dark rum to each mug.
5. Fill mugs the rest of the way with hot milk. Stir well, and dust with nutmeg.

# DEWBERRY MARGARITAS

## DYEING SEASON, BOOK 5

INGREDIENTS:

*Dewberry or Blackberry Puree*

- 2 pints fresh dewberries or blackberries
- 1/4 cup sugar
- Juice of 1/2 lime

*Lime Sugar*

- 2 cups sugar
- Zest of 3 limes
- 1 lime wedge

*Margaritas*

- 2 cups tequila
- 1/2 cup triple sec
- 1/2 cup sugar
- 2 limes

- Ice

DIRECTIONS:

1. *For the puree:* Add the berries to a medium saucepan with the sugar and lime juice. Cook over low heat, covered, 20 to 25 minutes. Strain using a fine mesh strainer, pressing the berries to extract as much juice/puree as possible. Place in the fridge to cool completely.
2. *For the lime sugar:* Mix together the sugar and lime zest. Use a piece of lime to moisten the rim of each margarita glass, and then dip in the lime sugar.
3. *For the margaritas:* In a blender, add 1 cup of the tequila, 1/4 cup of the triple sec, 1/4 cup of the sugar, and the juice of 1 lime. Fill the blender with ice and blend until smooth. Then add as much blackberry puree as desired, 1/3 to 1/2 cup.
4. Pour into 4 rimmed glasses and serve immediately. Repeat with the rest of the ingredients for the other 4 glasses.

# SAUCES

# VERDE SAUCE

INGREDIENTS:

- 2 pounds fresh tomatillos
- 2 cups yellow onions, minced
- 1 teaspoon fresh garlic, minced
- 1/4 cup fresh cilantro, minced
- 1 teaspoon fresh jalapeño, seeded and minced
- 1 tablespoon fresh oregano, minced
- Pinch of sugar
- 1/2 teaspoon salt
- 2 cups water

DIRECTIONS:

1. Place whole tomatillos in a sink full of hot water and allow to sit for 15 minutes while skins loosen. Remove skins.
2. Put tomatillos and remaining ingredients in a large, heavy

stock pot. Bring water to a boil. Lower heat. Simmer for 1 hour, stirring occasionally.
3. Puree in small batches in a blender or food processor until smooth.

# RED CHILI SAUCE

## MISTLETOE MURDER, BOOK 4

INGREDIENTS:

- 15 large dried chilies (such as Anaheim, New Mexico, California, or pasilla)
- 4–5 garlic cloves
- 2 teaspoons ground cumin
- 1 teaspoon salt
- 2 teaspoons all-purpose flour
- 2 teaspoons olive oil

DIRECTIONS:

1. Remove stems and seeds from dried chili peppers, and place peppers in a single layer on a baking sheet.
2. Roast in a 350°F oven for 2 to 5 minutes or until you smell a sweet roasted aroma, checking often to avoid burning.
3. Remove the chilies from oven and soak in enough hot water to cover for about 30 minutes or until cool.

4. Put peppers and 2½ cups of the soaking water into a blender (save the remaining soaking water); add garlic, cumin, and salt, then cover and blend until smooth.
5. In a 2-quart saucepan, stir flour into oil or melted shortening over medium heat until browned.
6. Carefully stir in blended chili mixture.
7. Simmer uncovered for 5 to 10 minutes or until slightly thickened. (If sauce gets too thick, stir in up to 1 cup of the remaining soaking water until you reach the desired thickness.)

Note: When working with chilies, use rubber gloves to protect your skin, and avoid contact with your eyes. Wash hands thoroughly with soap and water to remove all the chili oils.

# JAMS

# KILLER DEWBERRY JAM

## KILLER JAM, BOOK 1

Note: If you can't get Texas dewberries, blackberries work well, too!

INGREDIENTS:

- 1 lb. dewberries or blackberries
- ½ cup water
- 2 tablespoons lemon juice
- 1/4 large cooking apple, grated
- 1 lb. granulated sugar
- 1 vanilla pod

DIRECTIONS:

1. Sterilize four 8-ounce jam jars and put a small plate in the freezer, then wash the dewberries (or blackberries) and put into a heavy-bottomed pan with the water and lemon juice; add grated apple into the pan.

2. Bring mixture to a boil over a medium heat, and simmer for 5 minutes.
3. Add the sugar, stirring gradually until all the crystals have dissolved, then scrape the seeds from the vanilla pod into the jam, and stir. Increase the heat and boil until a candy thermometer consistently reads 220 degrees.
4. To test the jam to see if it's set, drop a little jam onto the frozen plate; when jam has set, the liquid will be gel, not liquid, when touched with a finger. If jam is still liquid, continue to boil for a few more minutes, then test again.
5. When set, pour the jam into sterilized jars, leaving a little bit of space at the top of the jar, and screw lids onto the jars while the jam is still hot. As they cool, the jar tops should 'pop,' indicating the seal is good. Leave jam jars untouched for at least 24 hours to help the jam set. (You can put the scraped vanilla bean in a mason jar with a cup of sugar to make vanilla sugar!)

## SPICED PUMPKIN BUTTER

### DEADLY BREW, BOOK 3

*(with thanks to Chloe Shepard)*

INGREDIENTS:

- 1 lb. sugar pumpkin or 15 oz. pureed pumpkin
- ½ cup apple cider
- 1 cup brown sugar
- 2 tbs maple syrup
- ½ tsp ground ginger
- ¼ tsp ground cloves
- ¼ tsp ground nutmeg
- 1 tsp ground cinnamon

DIRECTIONS:

1. If using fresh pumpkin, cut the pumpkin into pieces, removing seeds and stringy parts, and remove the stem and "butt." Place pumpkin, skin side down, on a baking sheet

and bake at 325 degrees for about an hour. Let cool. Remove the skin and puree the pumpkin in a food processor, adding a small amount of water if needed.
2. Mix pumpkin and remaining ingredients together in a large saucepan. Bring mixture to a full boil over medium-high heat. Reduce heat and continue cooking ten to fifteen minutes or until thickened, stirring frequently. Remove from heat. When slightly cooled, spoon into clean jars and refrigerate.

## SPICED PEAR JAM

### FATAL FROST, BOOK 2

INGREDIENTS:

- 8 cups chopped or coarsely ground peeled pears (about 5 1/2 pounds)
- 4 cups sugar
- 1 teaspoon ground cinnamon
- 1/4 teaspoon ground cloves

DIRECTIONS:

1. Combine all ingredients in a large, thick saucepan or Dutch oven. Simmer, uncovered, for 1-1/2 to 2 hours until jam sets (see below), stirring occasionally. Stir more frequently as the mixture thickens.
2. When jam has set, remove from heat and skim off foam. Carefully ladle into sterilized, hot half-pint jars, leaving 1/4-in. headspace. Remove air bubbles with a sterilized knife or spatula, then and wipe rims and adjust lids. Process

jars for 10 minutes in a boiling-water canner (Lucy uses a rack placed in a big stock pot). Yield: 6 half-pints.

*How to tell if jam is set:*

PUT a plate in the freezer for about fifteen minutes. When jam has thickened and seems like it might be ready, put a spoonful of hot jam on the plate, then push your finger through it. If the surface wrinkles and the jam doesn't flood back in to fill the gap, the jam has set. If it's not ready, turn the pan back on, simmer for five minutes and test again.

# CHEESES

# GRANDMA VOGEL'S COTTAGE CHEESE

## KILLER JAM, BOOK 1

INGREDIENTS:

- 1 gallon milk
- 3/4 cup white vinegar
- 1 1/2 teaspoons kosher salt

DIRECTIONS:

1. Pour milk into a large saucepan and place over medium heat until it reaches 120 degrees. Remove the milk from the heat and gently pour in the vinegar, stirring slowly for 1 to 2 minutes until the curd separates from the whey. Cover the mixture and allow it to sit at room temperature for 30 minutes.
2. Line a colander with a tea towel, then pour the mixture into the lined colander and allow it to sit and drain for 5 minutes. Gather up the edges of the cloth and rinse the curds under cold water for 3 to 5 minutes until they are

completely cooled, squeezing and moving the mixture as you rinse.
3. Once the curds are cool, squeeze them until they are as dry as possible and transfer them to a mixing bowl.
4. Add the salt and stir to combine, breaking up the curd into bite-size pieces as you go. Eat or refrigerate immediately.

# FARM-FRESH MOZZARELLA CHEESE

## WICKED HARVEST, BOOK 6

INGREDIENTS:

- 1 gallon milk, NOT ultra-pasteurized
- 1 1/2 tsp citric acid
- 1/4 rennet tablet or 1/4 tsp single strength liquid rennet
- 1 tsp cheese salt (adjust to taste). Kosher and sea salt work, too!

DIRECTIONS:

1. Clear your work area of all food, wipe it down, and use antibacterial cleaner before starting.
2. Crush 1/4 tablet of rennet and dissolve in 1/4 cup of cool non-chlorinated water, or add 1/4 tsp single strength liquid rennet to the water. Set aside to use later. Add 1 1/2 tsp. of citric acid to 1 cup cool water and pour into a large pot, then quickly add cold milk and mix it in well.
3. Heat the milk slowly until it reaches 90°F. (As the

temperature approaches 90°F, you may notice the milk beginning to curdle slightly). If the milk doesn't seem to be separating and forming a curd, you may need to increase this temp to 95°F or even 100F.

4. At 90°F (or when curds are properly formed—I'd recommend googling a picture), remove the pot from the burner and slowly add the prepared rennet to the milk. Stir from top to bottom for approximately 30 seconds, then stop. Cover the pot and leave it undisturbed for 5 minutes.
5. After 5 minutes, check the curd. It should look like custard, with a clear separation between the curds and whey. If the curd is too soft or the whey looks milky, let it sit for longer, up to 30 additional minutes.
6. Using a long knife, cut the curds into a 1" checkerboard pattern, then place the pot back on the stove and heat the curds to 105°F while slowly stirring them with your ladle. Take the pot off the burner and continue stirring slowly for 2-5 minutes; the longer you stir, the firmer the cheese.
7. With a slotted spoon, scoop curds into a colander and press the curd gently with your hand, pouring off as much whey as possible. (Rubber gloves help with the heat.)
8. From the colander, transfer the curds to a heat- and microwave-safe bowl, mix one teaspoon of salt into the curds, and microwave the curd for 1 minute. Drain off additional whey, then work the cheese with a spoon or your hands until it is cool enough to touch (again, rubber gloves will help). Microwave the curds twice more for 35 seconds each, repeating the kneading and draining each time.
9. Knead the curd as you would bread dough; after a few minutes, remove the curd from the bowl and continue kneading until the curd smooth and shiny. (If it cools before it reaches this point, put it in the microwave in increments of 15 seconds to heat it back up.) When the cheese is soft and pliable enough to stretch, if you feel it needs it, add a bit more salt, then stretch the cheese like taffy (you'll want to

do this many times) to create the fibers that make it mozzarella.
10. Knead the cheese back into a big ball until it is smooth and shiny. To cool it quickly, place it in a bowl of ice water and refrigerate. When cheese is cold, it will last for several days wrapped in plastic, but is best when eaten fresh. (Preferably with homegrown tomatoes and basil. Mmm.)

# CRAFTS

# MASON JAR BEESWAX CANDLES

## KILLER JAM, BOOK 1

INGREDIENTS:

- 1.5 pounds filtered beeswax
- 1 cup coconut oil
- 40 inches of cotton wick
- wick clip or clear tape
- 8 six-ounce candle jars
- double boiler
- Candy thermometer
- 8 popsicle sticks, pencils, or pens

DIRECTIONS:

1. Cut a length of wick that is about 2 inches longer than the height of your jar.
2. Tie the wick around a pencil and position the wick over the center of the jar. Use a wick clip to keep the wick on the bottom of the jar, or simply tape it down with clear tape.

3. Turn the stove to low, and melt the wax in a double boiler. When the beeswax is liquified, add coconut oil and stir until everything is melted and combined, and heat to 165 degrees.
4. Pour a thin layer of beeswax in the bottom of your jar, making sure some of it covers the end of the wick. Push the tip of the wick into place with your finger or the end of a pen or popsicle stick, then pull on the wick so that it hardens in an upright position (this will take 60 seconds or less).
5. When the wick has set, pour the rest of the hot wax into the jar, leaving 1/2 or 3/4" of space at the top of the jar, and check the position of the wick to make sure it is centered. Continue with remaining jars.
6. Allow the candles to harden for 24 hours, then trim the wicks to about 1/4 inch and allow it to set for another 24 hours before using.
7. Light the candle at the base of the wick so that some of wax is drawn up into the wick. (Tip: for longer-lasting candles, burn until wax melts all the way to the edge of the jar before extinguishing the flame.)

## MARY JANE'S LAVENDER GOAT MILK SOAP

### FATAL FROST, BOOK 2

INGREDIENTS:

- 12 ounces coconut oil
- 15 ounces olive oil
- 13 ounces palm oil or vegetable shortening
- 13 ounces goat milk, frozen for at least 24 hours
- 6 ounces lye
- 1 ounce lavender oil
- pH strips for testing

DIRECTIONS:

1. Break up frozen goat milk into chunks and pour into a large glass or stainless steel bowl. Then put the bowl in a sink that is half full with cold water and ice (it is important that the milk remains very cold).
2. Very slowly, add lye and "mash" it into the milk with a fork or stainless steel potato masher. Keep adding the lye until it

is all incorporated, replacing the ice in the sink if it melts so that milk/lye solution stays very cold. The milk may turn orange or even tan to light brown, but if it turns dark brown, you will have to discard it and start over.
3. When the mixture is ready, keep it on ice while you heat the oils. Measure them on a kitchen scale, then heat them slightly, until they are about 110° – 125°F.
4. When the oils are ready, slowly pour the lye/milk mixture into them. Mix by hand for the first 5 minutes, and then use an immersion blender until the consistency is like cake batter or pudding. When it comes to a trace (everything has emulsified and there aren't any streaks), add your essential oils and any additives and pour it into molds.
5. Wait 24 hours or more, then remove from molds and cut if desired. Let it cure for 3-4 weeks, turning the soap every so often so all sides have been exposed to air. The pH needs to drop to 8-10 so that it is gentle on skin. You can test the pH with test strips Wrap when completely cured.

Notes:

- Always keep goat milk frozen and the lye/milk mixture cold to keep it from scorching (turning dark brown)
- Lye is caustic and can burn your skin. Wear long sleeves, gloves, and goggles (if you have them) and keep a bit of white vinegar handy in case you get any on your skin (the vinegar will neutralize the lye).
- Use only stainless steel or glass bowls as plastic can pick up smells.

# NATURAL EASTER EGG DYES

## DYEING SEASON, BOOK 5

Although Lucy used dried ingredients like turmeric for her dye packets, you can easily whip up natural dyes at home.

RED – Mix 2 cups of grated raw beets with 1 tablespoon of vinegar. Boil with 2 cups of water for about 15 minutes (other options include frozen cranberries and strong Red Zinger tea).

YELLOW TO GOLD – Simmer 3 large handfuls of yellow/brown onion skins in 3 cups of water for about 15 minutes. Alternately, boil 2 or 3 tablespoons of ground turmeric or chamomile in 2 cups of water for about 15 minutes.

*Blue* – Boil 1 pound of crushed frozen blueberries in 2-3 cups of water for about 15 minutes. For lavender shades, use three cups of red cabbage leaves instead.

Notes:

Make the individual dyes in 3 different nonreactive saucepans. For a uniform color, strain the dye mixtures through cheesecloth or a fine strainer. If you prefer mottled, or tie-dyed eggs, leave the ingredients in the pan with the cooked beets, onion skins, or blueberries, then put the eggs directly in the pan to soak with the cooked ingredients. (The longer you soak the eggs the deeper the color will be.) You can also experiment by combining the different dyes in coffee cups to get different colors. To make designs, use a white crayon prior to dyeing.

# HONEY LIP BALM

## DEWBERRY FARM BONUS RECIPE

INGREDIENTS:

- 1 tsp beeswax
- ½ tsp honey
- 2 tsp almond oil
- 4 drops Vitamin E oil (optional)
- 2 drops Lemon or orange essential oil (optional)

DIRECTIONS:

1. Melt beeswax and honey in a double boiler or in a heat-proof jar or bowl if using microwave. When the wax and honey are just melted, remove from microwave or burner and whisk in almond oil and Vitamin E oil if using.
2. Pour the mixture into containers and allow to cool fully. For citrus-flavored lip balm, add a few drops of lemon or orange essential oil while whisking.

# GRANDMA VOGEL'S LAVENDER BATH SALTS

## DEWBERRY FARM BONUS RECIPE

INGREDIENTS:

- 1 cup Epsom salts
- 4 cups coarse sea salt or Kosher salt
- 1 cup baking soda
- 1 cup powdered milk (optional)
- 12 drops lavender essential oil
- 4 tablespoons lavender buds (optional)

DIRECTIONS:

1. Mix all together and store in Mason jars or Tupperware away from direct light.
2. Add 3/4-1 cup to warm bath water.

NOTE: For sore muscles, reverse the sea salt/Epsom salt ratio!

# KITCHEN TIPS

## LUCY'S HANDY KITCHEN TIPS

- To keep a pot from boiling over, put a little oil on a paper towel and wipe the inside rim.
- For bad smells in the kitchen, put a bowl of white vinegar out for a day or two. A bowl of fresh ground coffee also works.
- To keep cut herbs fresh, store them in damp paper towels in a sealed container in the refrigerator; alternately, trim the bottoms under running water and put the herbs in a glass filled with water and store in the refrigerator.
- To have homemade broth on hand when you need it, freeze broth in half-pint Tupperware or plastic containers, then remove the frozen broth and store in Ziplock bags.
- To defrost meat quickly, lay it on an aluminum cookie sheet; this conducts heat quickly and thaws the meat fast!
- To peel garlic, smash it with the flat of a French Chef's knife, then remove the peel easily.
- Save hard cheese rinds and freeze them; you can use them for great flavor in soups and stocks!
- Eggs are often good well past their "sell-by" dates! To test,

simply pop an egg in a bowl of water. If it floats, it's gone bad. If it stays at the bottom of the bowl, it's still good!
- To slice cakes (as in dividing one cake into two layers) or make neat rounds of soft cheese (like goat cheese) neatly, use unscented dental floss; just wrap it around the cheese or cake you're slicing, then pull the ends toward each other and keep pulling until you have a perfect slice! (You can use toothpicks to mark the middle of a cake and make sure you don't end up with lopsided layers.
- To get more juice out of lemons, limes, and oranges, roll them while putting pressure on them with the palm of your hand before juicing.
- To liquefy honey that has crystallized, simply pop the jar in a pot of hot water and let it melt.
- For fresh-smelling laundry, put a few drops of essential oil (like lavender) onto a paper towel and toss it into the dryer.

# GARDEN TIPS

# LUCY AND GRANDMA VOGEL'S GARDEN TIPS

Vegetable gardening is so rewarding; there's nothing better than eating food you grew yourself, and lettuce straight from your own garden is tender and delicious and bears little to no resemblance to the stuff you buy at the grocery store. (And we all know that home-grown tomatoes are transcendent.) Here are some of my (and Grandma Vogel's) tips to get you started on your green adventure!

## KNOW YOUR AREA

Different parts of the country have different planting times; here in Texas, we have a cool season and a hot season, and things that northern gardeners would plant in spring, we plant in the fall. Some veggies do better as transplants, others as seeds; lettuce does well direct-sowed, but tomato plants do better as transplants started in pots. Find out the timing, planting method, and vegetable varieties best adapted for your area for maximum yield.

## SOIL

Soil is the most important part of gardening. Compost is a great way to enrich soil, but it's always a good idea to have your soil tested so you can amend pH, etc. And always keep adding organic matter to your garden. It'll keep it productive! (If you can, though, add compost two to three weeks before planting so it has time to integrate into the soil.)

If you have diseased plants, pull them out and pick up any leaves from the soil before disposing of them somewhere other than your compost pile to prevent reinfection of next year's plants.

It's also good to rotate plants and plant families in the garden. If you have one section dedicated to nightshades (tomatoes, eggplants, peppers, and/or potatoes) and another for cucurbits (melons, squash, and cucumbers), for example, try not to replant the same plot with plants in the same family two years in a row. Change things up so that pests from last year don't have a chance to put down roots, so to speak. (Also, beans are nitrogen fixers; if the plants are healthy, they're a great addition to the compost pile, or just till them into the soil; it will give next year's plants a boost.) Healthy soil will grow healthy plants that are resistant to disease and pests. It all starts with good soil.

Earthworms are great for your garden, and if you see lots of them, you'll know your soil health is good. These garden helpers aerate the soil and leave wormcastings, which are garden gold, in their wake. (Another reason to go organic; it will help your earthworm population thrive.)

## WATERING

Water your garden early in the morning, before the sun is hot. Watering at night can encourage powdery mildew or other fungal problems to develop. Adding more organic material to the soil will greatly increase its ability to retain water, so make sure you're amending your soil regularly!

Also, particularly if you live in a place like Texas, which is prone to drought, it is better to water less frequently and more deeply to encourage deep roots. And if you have tomatoes, a soaker hose is the best way to go; splashing water on leaves can cause disease to spread.

## CREATING A NEW PLOT

To turn a grassy area into a new plot, one method is to cover it with black plastic for several weeks or months (this works particularly well in summer). The plastic will bake the grass. Another method is to cover the grass with a thick layer of newspaper, then put several inches of compost and soil on top of it, followed by another layer of newspaper, more compost, and mulch to hold it all down. Water frequently as the organic material breaks down.

Give it a few months, refreshing with more newspaper and compost as needed, then turn up your new plot with a spade, and you should be good to go!

## SMALL-SPACE GARDENING

If you want a garden but don't have much space, trellis your vining vegetables! Cucumbers, squash, melons, and even tomatoes are great candidates for this; you can support heavy melons by wrapping stockings around them and tying them to the trellis. (This will also be a source of amusement to your neighbors.) To train cucumber plants and keep them from taking over the world, or at least your garden, it's good to remove any dead leaves and also the "suckers," or shoots the shoots that come out from the main stem. Removing dead leaves and suckers will also improve air circulation and help light reach the leaves.

## GO ORGANIC

Wherever you can, use natural fertilizers and pesticides to keep your garden healthy. Your plants, your soil, and your health will thank you!

## WEEDING

Early is better. I like to mix in compost, then go over the area with a hoe once any seeds hidden in the soil (usually weeds) have sprouted, then water it and let it sit for a few days before going after it with a hoe again. This gets rid of some of the weed seed bank in the garden and makes life easier later in the season.

It's best to go after weeds frequently, while they're small; this is easily done with a hoe that disrupts the fragile roots (be careful not to get your veggies in the process). If weeds do take hold (and they do sometimes—life does get in the way), try to make sure you get them before they go to seed, or you'll have that many more to deal with next year!

## PLANTING A PEST BARRIER

Plant onions, chives, or garlic around the perimeter of the garden. Not only are they a tasty addition to all kinds of dishes, but insects HATE them. (In Texas, we plant garlic cloves in the fall and enjoy "green garlic" in winter and spring; it looks like scallions, but has a lovely mild garlic taste and is terrific in salads and pasta dishes.)

## TOMATO TIPS

Pick tomato varieties that work well for your area; in Texas, big tomatoes like beefsteak are hard to grow, but cherry tomatoes and plants that mature quickly (like Early Girl and Celebrity) do well. I like to plant several varieties each year, because some types always outperform others, and it varies from year to year. To get a jumpstart on tomato plants in the spring (and protect them from freezes and insect invasions), wrap the cages in white landscape cloth, sealing the tops with clothespins. It'll keep the bugs out and your plants warm! (And be sure to plant the tomatoes deep; Grandma Vogel always covered the first set of leaves with dirt, to make the plant extra sturdy and strong, then made a small trough all around the plant to retain water.)

For an extra boost, dissolve one or two tablespoons of Epsom salts in a gallon of water and water your plants!

And don't forget; tomatoes don't set fruit if the temperature is above 90 degrees, so plant them as early as you can, particularly if you live in a warm climate. Marigolds are a great companion plant for tomatoes, and they're beautiful, too.

## PLANTING A SALAD GARDEN

In Texas, lettuce is a cool-season crop (we plant it in fall), but instead of planting lines, it can be fun to just dedicate an area to lettuce and broadcast the seed—I like to use a lettuce mix so I've got a variety of types in the salad bowl. Snails can be a problem; if this is the case, go out at night with a flashlight, collect them all, and relocate them. You may have to do this a few times (and replant with fresh seed); in Buttercup, we plant, spend a few nights collecting snails, and then sprinkle an organic snail bait such as Sluggo before resowing seed.

Usually by the second or third planting, the snail population is reduced enough to let the lettuce grow. All winter long, instead of pulling up lettuces, we go snip leaves as needed and let the plant continue to regenerate. (Once the weather warms up and the lettuce flowers, or "bolts," you'll want to pull it, though; lettuce turns bitter once it's flowered.)

## PEST CONTROL

Check your garden frequently for problems; if you catch things in the early stages, they are usually much easier to control. Snip off mildewed leaves immediately and dispose of them, then treat the rest of the plant with an organic fungicide, for example. If you have aphids, spray the plants with a hard spray of water each morning and consider doubling down with an organic pesticide. (I once vacuumed up several hundred baby stink bugs with a Dustbuster, then left the Dustbuster in the laundry room without emptying it first. You can guess what happened next.)

A few years back, I managed a potentially catastrophic mealy bug infestation by ordering a special mealy-bug-eating ladybug. I put translucent landscape cloth over the infested area, clipped the cloth together with clothespins and sealed the edges with stakes, then released the ladybugs inside. They hung out under the cloth and reproduced before escaping, and the baby ladybugs (which are flightless and look nothing like adult ladybugs) cleaned up all the mealybugs in record time, with no chemicals needed.

If you're short on ladybugs, which you can usually buy at garden stores, incidentally), a good all-purpose organic pesticide you can make at home is garlic-pepper tea. Turn the page for Grandma Vogel's easy-to-make recipe.

Above all, have fun, be sure to plant several varieties of veggies in case part of your garden has a catastrophic failure, and if you don't love eggplant, don't plant a whole row of it. (I speak from experience.)

# GRANDMA VOGEL'S GARLIC-PEPPER TEA

Kills aphids, stink bugs, and other garden pests naturally! This recipe will make 1 gallon of Garlic Pepper Tea Concentrate.

INGREDIENTS:

- 2 bulbs garlic
- 2 jalapeno peppers
- 1 tablespoon Castile soap

DIRECTIONS:

1. Take 2 bulbs of garlic and 2 jalapeno (or other hot) peppers and toss them into a blender.
2. Fill the blender jar a little over half-way with water. Put the lid on the blender and blend on high. It isn't a bad idea to wear rubber gloves and some sort of glasses or goggles to protect your eyes. This is powerful stuff, folks.
3. Blend until it turns to liquid and strain the solids with

cheesecloth. You will now Pour the tea into a clean 1 gallon milk jug, add Castile soap, and fill to the top with water.
4. To use, simply pour into a spray bottle and use on your plants! (I like to do this in the evening, after the sun has gone down, or on a cloudy day so I don't burn the leaves.)

# SNEAK PEEK: KILLER JAM

## CHAPTER ONE

I've always heard it's no use crying over spilled milk. But after three days of attempting to milk Blossom the cow (formerly Heifer #82), only to have her deliver a well-timed kick that deposited the entire contents of my bucket on the stall floor, it was hard not to feel a few tears of frustration forming in the corners of my eyes.

Stifling a sigh, I surveyed the giant puddle on the floor of the milking stall and reached for the hose. I'd tried surrounding the bucket with blocks, holding it in place with my feet—even tying the handle to the side of the stall with a length of twine. But for the sixth straight time, I had just squeezed the last drops from the teats when Blossom swung her right rear hoof in a kind of bovine hook kick, walloping the top of the bucket and sending gallons of the creamy white fluid spilling across both the concrete floor and my boots. I reprimanded her, but she simply tossed her head and grabbed another mouthful of the feed I affectionately called "cow chow."

She looked so unassuming. So velvety-nosed and kind, with big, long-lashed eyes. At least she had on the day I'd selected her from the line of cows for sale at the Double-Bar Ranch. Despite all the reading I'd done on selecting a heifer, when she pressed her soft nose up against my cheek, I knew she belonged at Dewberry Farm. Thankfully, the rancher I'd purchased her from had seemed more than happy to let her go, extolling her good nature and excellent production.

He'd somehow failed to mention her phobia of filled buckets.

Now, as I watched the tawny heifer gamboling into the pasture beside my farmhouse, kicking her heels up in what I imagined was a cow's version of the middle finger, I took a deep breath and tried to be philosophical about the whole thing. She still had those big brown eyes, and it made me happy to think of her in my pasture rather than the cramped conditions at Double-Bar Ranch. And she'd only kicked the milk bucket, not me.

Despite the farm's growing pains, as I turned toward the farmhouse, I couldn't help but smile. After fifteen years of life in Houston, I now lived in a century-old yellow farmhouse—the one I'd dreamed of owning my whole life—with ten acres of rolling pasture and field, a peach orchard, a patch of dewberries, and a quaint, bustling town just up the road. The mayor had even installed a Wi-Fi transmitter on the water tower, which meant I could someday put up a website for the farm. So what if Blossom was more trouble than I'd expected, I told myself. I'd only been a dairy farmer for seventy-two hours; how could I expect to know everything?

In fact, it had only been six months since my college roommate, Natalie Barnes, had convinced me to buy the farm that had once belonged to my grandparents. Natalie had cashed in her chips a few years back and bought an inn in Maine, and I'd never seen her happier. With my friend's encouragement, I'd gone after the dream of reliving those childhood summers, which I'd spent fishing in the creek and learning to put up jam at my grandmother's elbow.

It had been a long time since those magical days in Grandma Vogel's steamy, deliciously scented kitchen. I'd spent several years as a reporter for the *Houston Chronicle*, fantasizing about a simpler life as I wrote about big-city crime and corruption. As an antidote to the heartache I'd seen in my job, I'd grown tomatoes in a sunny patch of the backyard, made batches of soap on the kitchen stove, and even kept a couple of chickens until the neighbors complained.

Ever since those long summer days, I'd always fantasized about living in Buttercup, but it wasn't until two events happened almost simultaneously that my dream moved from fantasy to reality. First, the paper I worked for, which like most newspapers was suffering from the onset of the digital age, laid off half the staff, offering me a buyout that, combined with my savings and the equity on my small house, would give me a nice nest egg. And second, as I browsed the web one day, I discovered that my grandmother's farm—which she'd sold fifteen years ago, after my grandfather passed—was up for sale.

Ignoring my financial advisor's advice—and fending off questions from friends who questioned my sanity—I raided the library for every homesteading book I could find, cobbled together a plan I hoped would keep me from starving, took the buyout from the paper, and put an offer in on Dewberry Farm. Within a month, I went from being Lucy Resnick, reporter, to Lucy Resnick, unemployed homesteader of my grandparents' derelict farm. Now, after months of backbreaking work, I surveyed the rows of fresh green lettuce and broccoli plants sprouting up in the fields behind the house with a deep sense of satisfaction. I might not be rich, and I might not know how to milk a cow, but I was living the life I'd always wanted.

I focused on the tasks for the day, mentally crossing cheese making off the list as I headed for the little yellow farmhouse. There might not be fresh mozzarella on the menu, but I did have two more batches of soap to make, along with shade cover to spread over the lettuce, cucumber seeds to plant, chickens to feed, and buckets of dewberries to pick and turn into jam. I also needed to stop by and pick up some beeswax from the Bees' Knees, owned by local beekeeper Nancy Shaw.

The little beeswax candles I made in short mason jars were a top seller at Buttercup Market Days, and I needed to make more.

Fortunately, it was a gorgeous late spring day, with late bluebonnets carpeting the roadsides and larkspur blanketing the meadow beside the house, the tall flowers' ruffled lavender and pink spikes bringing a smile to my face. They'd make beautiful bouquets for the market this coming weekend—and for the pitcher in the middle of my kitchen table. Although the yellow Victorian-style farmhouse had been neglected and left vacant for the past decade or more, many of my grandmother's furnishings remained. She hadn't been able to take them with her to the retirement home, and for some reason, nobody else had claimed or moved them out, so many things I remembered from my childhood were still there.

The house had good bones, and with a bit of paint and elbow grease, I had quickly made it a comfortable home. The white tiled countertop sparkled again, and my grandmother's pie safe with its punched tin panels was filled with jars of jam for the market. I smoothed my hand over the enormous pine table my grandmother had served Sunday dinners on for years. I'd had to work to refinish it, sanding it down before adding several layers of polyurethane to the weathered surface, but I felt connected to my grandmother every time I sat down to a meal.

The outside had taken a bit more effort. Although the graceful oaks still sheltered the house, looking much like they had when I had visited as a child, the line of roses that lined the picket fence had suffered from neglect, and the irises were lost in a thicket of Johnson grass. The land itself had been in worse shape; the dewberries the farm had been named for had crept up into where the garden used to be, hiding in a sea of mesquite saplings and giant purple thistles. I had had to pay someone to plow a few acres for planting, and had lost some of the extra poundage I'd picked up at my desk job rooting out the rest. Although it was a continual battle against weeds, the greens I had put in that spring were looking lush and healthy—and the dewberries had been corralled to the banks of Dewberry Creek, which ran along the back side of the property. The peach trees in the small orchard had been cloaked in gorgeous pink blossoms and now were laden with tiny fruits. In a few short months, I'd be trying out the honey-peach preserves recipe I'd found in my grandmother's handwritten cookbook, which was my most treasured possession. Sometimes, when I flipped through its yellowed pages, I almost felt as if my grandmother were standing next to me.

Now, I stifled a sigh of frustration as I watched the heifer browse the pasture. With time, I was hoping to get a cheese concern going; right now, I only had Blossom, but hopefully she'd calve a heifer, and with luck, I'd have two or three milkers soon. Money was on the tight side, and I might have to consider driving to farmers' markets in Austin to make ends meet—or maybe finding some kind of part-time job—but now that I'd found my way to Buttercup, I didn't want to leave.

I readjusted my ponytail—now that I didn't need to dress for work, I usually pulled my long brown hair back in the mornings—and mentally reviewed my to-do list. Picking dewberries was next, a delightful change from the more mundane tasks of my city days. I needed a few more batches of jam for Buttercup's Founders' Day Festival and Jam-Off, which was coming up in a few days. I'd pick before it got too hot; it had been a few days since I'd been down by the creek, and I hoped to harvest another several quarts.

Chuck, the small apricot rescue poodle who had been my constant companion for the past five years, joined me as I grabbed a pair of gardening gloves and the galvanized silver bucket I kept by the back door, then headed past the garden in the back and down to the creek, where the sweet smell of sycamores filled the air. I didn't let Chuck near Blossom—I was afraid she would do the same thing to him that she did to the milk bucket—but he accompanied me almost everywhere else on the farm, prancing through the tall grass, guarding me from wayward squirrels and crickets, and—unfortunately—picking up hundreds of burrs. I'd had to shave him within a week of arriving at the farm, and I was still getting used to having a bald poodle. This morning, he romped through the tall grass, occasionally stopping to sniff a particularly compelling tuft of grass. His pink skin showed through his clipped fur, and I found myself wondering if there was such a thing as doggie sunscreen.

The creek was running well this spring—we'd had plenty of rain, which was always welcome in Texas, and a giant bullfrog plopped into the water as I approached the mass of brambles with their dark, sweet berries. They were similar to the blackberries I bought in the store, but a bit longer, with a sweet-tart tang that I loved. I popped the first few in my mouth.

I went to work filling the bucket, using a stick to push the brambles aside, and had filled it about halfway when I heard the grumble of a motor coming up the long driveway. Chuck, who had been trying to figure out how to get to the fish that were darting in the deeper part of the creek, turned and growled. I shushed him as we headed back toward the farmhouse, the bucket swinging at my side.

A lanky man in jeans and a button-down shirt was unfolding himself from the front seat of the truck as I opened the back gate. Chuck surged ahead of me, barking and growling, then slinking to my ankle when I shushed him with a sharp word.

"Can I help you?" I asked the man. He was in his mid-forties, with work-worn boots and the roughened skin of a man who'd spent most of his life outdoors.

"You Lucy Resnick?" he asked.

"I am," I said, putting down the bucket. Chuck growled again and put himself between us.

"Butch Simmons, Lone Star Exploration," the man said, squinting at me.

"Nice to meet you," I said, extending a hand. Chuck yipped, and I apologized.

"Good doggie," the man said, reaching down to let the poodle sniff him. Usually, that was all the little dog needed to become comfortable, but something about the man upset him. He growled, backing away.

"I don't know what's gotten into him," I said, scooping him up in my arms. "Can I help you with something?" I asked again, holding the squirming poodle tight.

"Mind if I take a few pictures? We're surveying the property before we start the exploration process."

"Exploration process?" I asked. "Didn't anyone tell you?"

"Tell me what?"

He turned his head and spit out a wad of snuff. I wrinkled my nose, revolted by the glob of brown goo on the caliche driveway. "We're drillin' for oil."

Want to find out what happens next? Download your copy of Killer Jam, the first Dewberry Farm mystery, now!

# MORE BOOKS BY KAREN MACINERNEY

To download a free book and receive members-only outtakes, giveaways, short stories, recipes, and updates, join Karen's Reader's Circle at www.karenmacinerney.com! You can also join her Facebook community; she often hosts giveaways and loves getting to know her readers there.

And don't forget to follow her on BookBub to get newsflashes on new releases!

**The Dewberry Farm Mysteries**
- *Killer Jam*
- *Fatal Frost*
- *Deadly Brew*
- *Mistletoe Murder*
- *Dyeing Season*
- *Wicked Harvest*
- *Dewberry Farm Mystery #7, Summer/Fall 2020*
- *Six Merry Little Murders: A Cozy Christmas Bundle featuring Slay Bells Ring, a Dewberry Farm Christmas Novella*
- *Lucy's Farmhouse Kitchen*

MORE BOOKS BY KAREN MACINERNEY

## The Gray Whale Inn Mysteries
*Murder on the Rocks*
*Dead and Berried*
*Murder Most Maine*
*Berried to the Hilt*
*Brush With Death*
*Death Runs Adrift*
*Whale of a Crime*
*Claws for Alarm*
*Scone Cold Dead*
*Anchored Inn (April 2020)*
*Cookbook: The Gray Whale Inn Kitchen*
*Blueberry Blues (A Gray Whale Inn Short Story)*
*Pumpkin Pied (A Gray Whale Inn Short Story)*
*Iced Inn (A Gray Whale Inn Short Story)*
*Lupine Lies (A Gray Whale Inn Short Story) (January 2020)*
*Four Seasons at the Gray Whale Inn: A Cozy Story Collection (January 2020)*

## The Margie Peterson Mysteries
*Mother's Day Out*
*Mother Knows Best*
*Mother's Little Helper*

## The Snug Harbor Mysteries
A new cozy Maine series set at Seaside Cottage Books in Snug Harbor, Maine. Books 1-3 coming early 2020!

## Tales of an Urban Werewolf
*Howling at the Moon*
*On the Prowl*
*Leader of the Pack*

## ACKNOWLEDGMENTS

First, many thanks to my family, not just for putting up with me, but for continuing to come up with creative ways to kill people. (You should see the looks we get in restaurants.)

Thank you also to the folks at Trianon Coffee for keeping me caffeinated and providing wonderful company and feedback... especially, you, Chloe Payne, and your darling Violet! (If you need a signed copy of a book for a gift and live in Austin, Trianon now carries them; thank you!)

Thanks always to the MacInerney Mystery Mavens, who are indispensable with all manner of things, from covers to concepts to early reads... what would I do without you? Thank you also to Kim Killion for her amazing cover art and to Angi Hegner for her formatting prowess :)

And finally, thank you to YOU, and to ALL of the wonderful readers who make Dewberry Farm possible, especially my fabulous Facebook community. You keep me going!

# ABOUT THE AUTHOR

Karen MacInerney is the USA Today bestselling author of multiple mystery series, and her victims number well into the double digits. She lives in Austin, Texas with her sassy family, Tristan, and Little Bit (a.k.a. Dog #1 and Dog #2).

Feel free to visit Karen's web site at www.karenmacinerney.com, where you can download a free book and sign up for her Readers' Circle to receive subscriber-only short stories, deleted scenes, recipes and other bonus material. You can also find her on Facebook (she spends an inordinate amount of time there), where Karen loves getting to know her readers, answering questions, and offering quirky, behind-the-scenes looks at the writing process (and life in general).

P. S. Don't forget to follow Karen on BookBub to get newsflashes on new releases!

www.karenmacinerney.com
karen@karenmacinerney.com

facebook.com/AuthorKarenMacInerney
twitter.com/KarenMacInerney

Made in the USA
Middletown, DE
14 July 2020